D1143327

EX LIBRIS

The Art of Being a Woman

My Mother, Schiaparelli and Me

PATRICIA
VOLK

HUTCHINSON
LONDON

Published by Hutchinson 2013

2 4 6 8 10 9 7 5 3 1

Grateful acknowledgment is made to the following for permission to reprint previously published material: Copper Canyon Press: Excerpt from "Gender Bender" by Jennifer Michael Hecht from *Who Said*. Originally published in *The New Yorker* (October 3, 2011). Copyright © 2011 by Jennifer Michael Hecht. Reprinted with the permission of The Permissions Company, Inc., on behalf of Copper Canyon Press, www.coppercanyonpress.org.

V&A Publishing: Excerpts from *Shocking Life: The Autobiography of Elsa Schiaparelli* by Elsa Schiaparelli. Reprinted by permission of V&A Enterprises, Ltd.

The illustration credits on pp.279–83 constitute an extension of this copyright page.

First published in the United States in 2013 by
Alfred A. Knopf, a division of Random House, Inc., New York,
and in Canada by Random House of Canada Limited, Toronto.

First published in Great Britain in 2013 by
Hutchinson
Random House, 20 Vauxhall Bridge Road,
London SW1V 2SA

www.windmill-books.co.uk

Addresses for companies within The Random House Group Limited can be found at: www.randomhouse.co.uk/offices.htm

The Random House Group Limited Reg. No. 954009

A CIP catalogue record for this book
is available from the British Library

ISBN 9780091944575

The Random House Group Limited supports the Forest Stewardship Council® (FSC®), the leading international forest-certification organisation. Our books carrying the FSC label are printed on FSC®-certified paper. FSC is the only forest-certification scheme supported by the leading environmental organisations, including Greenpeace. Our paper procurement policy can be found at: www.randomhouse.co.uk/environment

Printed and bound in Great Britain by Clays Ltd, St Ives Plc

FOR JACKSON MORGEN, SAMUEL VOLK

AND MILES BENJAMIN.

If you see a girl dressed to say

"No one tells me
what to do"

you know someone once told her what to do.

—Jennifer Michael Hecht

Contents

Audrey Elaine Morgen Volk.

Elsa Luisa Maria Schiaparelli.

The Art of Being a Woman

chapter one

Mirrors

Everything is mirrors. The legs of the vanity, the vanity itself, the pullout stool. The drawers, drawer pulls, the ivy planters on both ends. The three adjustable face-mirrors that recess behind beveled mirror frames.

Audrey wears her green velvet robe. It grazes her green carpet and matches her green drapes. A broad lace collar frames her face. When she perches on the stool we are almost the same height. I stand behind her to the left. That way I can watch from every angle. I can see her reflection in all three face-mirrors and see the real her too, her flesh-and-blood profile closest to me. I can see four different views of my mother simultaneously. Sometimes, when she adjusts the mirrors, I can see thousands of her, each face nesting a slightly smaller face. The lace vee of her robe gets tiny, tinier, smaller than a stamp, until it vanishes.

"Is there a word for that?" I ask.

"Phantasmagoria, darling," my mother says.

The mirrored drawers store her tools. The left drawer holds hair-grooming aids: a tortoiseshell comb, her rat tail, a brush, clips, bobby pins, hairpins, brown rubber curlers, perforated aluminum ones. In the middle drawer, she keeps her creams, tonics and astringents. (Soap is the enemy. She does not wash her face. Water touches it only when she swims.) A blue and white box of Kleenex, the cellophane tube of Co-ets (quilted disposable cotton pads), her tweezers, cuticle scissors and emery boards that are made, she has told me, out of crushed garnets, her birthstone. The right-hand drawer (she is right-handed) organizes makeup and—separated from everything else, in its own compartment, her eyelash curler.

Everybody tells me my mother is beautiful. The butcher tells me. The dentist, the doormen, my teachers, cab drivers gaping at her in the rearview mirror as they worry the wheel. Friends from school, friends from camp, camp counselors, the hostess at Schrafft's. The cashier at Rappaport's and the pharmacist at Whelan's, where we get Vicks VapoRub for growing pains. At Indian Walk, the salesman measures my feet for Mary Janes and says, "You have a very beautiful mother, little girl. Do you know that?" When a man tips his hat on Broadway and says, "Mrs. Volk! How lovely to see you!," my mother says, "Patty, this is Mr. Lazar, a customer of your father's." We shake hands. "How do you do, Mr. Lazar?" I say, or "Nice to meet you, Mr. Lazar," and Mr. Lazar pinches my cheek. "Did anybody ever tell you," he says, "you have one gorgeous mother?" Thursday nights, when four generations of family gather at my grandmother's for dinner, the relatives tell my mother, "You look so beautiful tonight, darling." Then they violate Audrey's Pronoun Rule: "It is rude to discuss someone who is present using the third person. Never call someone within hearing distance 'he' or 'she.' Refer to that person by name." Yet they use "she." They speak about my mother as if she weren't there. Right in front of her they say, "Isn't she beautiful? Did you ever in your life?"

But this face in the mirror right now, people who think my mother is beautiful don't know this face. I know what my mother looks like without makeup. I know her real face. I know how beautiful she really is.

She spreads two bobby pins with her teeth and pins her hair back. She dips three fingers in a large jar of Pond's, then creams her face in a circular motion. She plucks four Kleenexes:

FRRRIIIIP!
FRRRIIIIP!
FRRRIIIIP!
FRRRIIIIP!

and tissues off the Pond's. Here she sometimes pauses, meets my eyes in the mirror and says, "Never let a man see you with cold cream on your face." She disposes of remaining shininess using tonic shaken onto a Co-et. Her face is bare, the smooth sleeping face I kiss before leaving for school. Her poreless skin, stretched tight in flat planes, no matter what time of year it is, looks tan.

She dabs on moisturizer and smoothes it in. From the right-hand drawer, she extracts a white plastic box of Max Factor pancake makeup. Its contents are the color of a Band-Aid and smell like an attic. Sometimes she calls pancake her "base." Sometimes it's "my foundation." She unscrews the lid and rubs a moist sponge into the color. She makes five smears with the sponge: center of the forehead, both cheeks, tip of nose, chin. Then she begins the work of evening it out, concentrating to make sure the color reaches her hairline and under her chin, and that part of the nose dab is used to lighten the inside corners of her eyes. She is satisfied when her face is all one color, including her lips. This is the moment she stops looking like my mother. This is when her face is reduced to two eyes and two nostrils. It is as flat as the rink at Rockefeller Center. This is when I swear:

"I will never, ever wear makeup, Ma."

"You'll change your tune."

"I won't."

She laughs. "We'll see."

She slips her base back in the drawer and flips the lid on her cream rouge. She dots her cheekbones and feathers the color. Opening her compact, she pats on powder, focusing on her nose. She inspects herself from all angles. She taps on pale blue eye shadow with her pinky. Her red mascara-box slides open revealing a black cake and miniature toothbrush. She swirls the brush in a shot glass filled with water then rubs it against the cake. Holding the brush to her lashes, she blinks against it, upper lids first. She freshens her eyebrows with the brush, shaping them and making sure no powder lurks in the hairs. Then it is time for the eyelash curler. The bottom half looks like the grip of scissors. The working end is an eyelash guillotine. She brings the curler up to an eye. She rearranges her lipless mouth into a black "O." If she blinks or sneezes while curling her eyelashes, the eyelash curler will pull them out. Her eyes will be bald.

She leans so close to the mirror it mists. She opens her eyes wide, angling her lashes into the vise.

"Don't bump me," she warns.

We hold our breaths. She clamps down, setting the lashes. We exhale when she releases them and moves to the other eye.

Now she sits back a bit. She analyzes her work. My mother has painted a portrait of her face on top of her face. My mother is a painting. She takes the pins out of her hair and drops them in the pin drawer. She shakes her blondish hair out and fluffs her fingers through it. If it is Saturday, there's a chance her nails haven't chipped yet. She gets them done Fridays for the weekend and even though she is careful, sometimes they chip. When that happens, she blurts a woeful "Darn!" and it breaks my heart.

Finally, she is ready to apply her lipstick, the only color she wears: Elizabeth Arden's "Sky Blue Pink." Stretching a smile, my mother paints her lips back on. She mashes them together then blots them on a folded tissue:

FRRRIIIIP!

She reapplies the "Sky Blue Pink," blotting one last time.

"If you blot twice," she instructs, "you can eat a frankfurter and your lipstick still won't come off."

Once her lips pass inspection, she is ready to ask me to leave her room. Audrey does not wish to be seen getting dressed. She does not wish to be seen in her underthings. I have seen her in a bathing suit at the beach and once by accident in a full slip while waiting for her at the dressmaker's. I have never seen her body. My sister says when she's dead we'll strip her and see everything. I don't want to. One morning at breakfast, Audrey's bathrobe buckled between the buttons and I saw something she would not have wanted me to see. I was miserable.

She adjusts the mirrors and turns her face from side to side. She smiles, raises an eyebrow and flirts with herself. She inspects her teeth for lipstick. When she is satisfied, she reaches for one of the two bottles on top of her vanity. During the day, she opts for the larger one. This bottle is five and a half inches tall and filled with yellow eau de cologne. The top, electric pink, looks like Ali Baba's hat. The bottle has breasts. The woman who made the bottle, a sculptor named Leonor Fini, modeled it on the mannequin of a Hollywood movie star. The movie star's name is Mae West. In summer camp, we wear orange canvas flotation vests the RAF nick-named Mae Wests that make us look busty like the bottle. We pose like calendar girls with our hands behind our heads. Wiggling our hips we chant:

Knit one
Purl two
Mae West
Woo! Woo!

When she is going out for the evening, my mother uses the smaller version of the bottle. This one contains perfume the color of whiskey. It is three inches high and rests on a gold-and-pink velvet pedestal. The bottle is covered by a clear glass dome made in Bohemia, a miniature version of the kind taxidermists use to protect stuffed owls. White lace is printed around the base of the dome and it's raised, you can feel it with your fingertips. The neck of the bottle, where it meets the round gold head of the frosted-glass dauber, is wrapped with a choker of gold cord. The cord is sealed with a membrane called onionskin that rips the first time the bottle is used. Draped over the cord is a minuscule measuring tape made of cloth. It hangs from behind the mannequin's neck and crosses over the front of the bottle where a navel would be. Here a small metallic seal with the letter "S" in the center

holds the tape together. Tucked under the
of the frosted dauber are glass flowers—baby
yellow, and sometimes dark blue—with conti
stamens and two green glass leaves, all hand-blo ne
island of Murano. The flowers are pierced by wires covered with green florist's tape and twisted into a nosegay until the stems join in a point.

The bottle, its dome and its pedestal are packaged in a box that opens like a bound book. Its green velvet spine is stamped in gold with the name of the perfume and the woman who made it, the perfume's title and author. The perfume and its box are called a "perfume presentation." You could slip the presentation between two books on a shelf and no one would know it wasn't a book. My mother says the perfume is manufactured in a mansion not far from Paris. She says each bottle has twenty separate parts made in three different countries and takes thirty ladies to assemble. My mother touches the long frosted dauber to her pulse points—the places blood flows closest to the skin, hence her warmest external places, where the scent heats most and disperses widest—the inside of her wrists, behind her ears, and the backs of her knees. In the evening, if she is going out, she dabs below her neck.

When she leaves the apartment, I play games with the bottle. I dress up in her green velvet robe, lift the flowers out of the measuring tape and pretend a man is giving them to me: "Why, monsieur! *Merci* for zee lovely bouquet! Ooo-la-la!" I pretend I am selling the bottle to a famous customer in my fancy French store: "Madame would perhaps care to buy zee perfume, *oui oui*?" or that the bottle is a movie star and she needs my opinion.

The name of the perfume is "Shocking." It is made by Elsa Schiaparelli (SKI-AH-PA-*RAY*-LEE). I know it is special. Every year on my mother's birthday, my father gives it to her, every January 21 the same gift. Late at night, after closing our family's restaurant, he opens the door to our bedroom. "Get up, girls!" He shakes my sister and me awake. We follow him down the hall, past the locked linen closet, into their bedroom so we can witness the event. Every year my mother is surprised. Every year she is thrilled.

"Oh, Cecil!" She clasps her hands under her chin. "Really, you are much too extravagant!"

She throws her arms around his neck and kisses him. She raises one foot behind her, pointing her toe like she does when they dance. She balances against him, smiling down at her daughters. "Girls, I hope you know: Your father is the most generous man in the world!"

Then my father says to us: "Isn't your mother the most beautiful woman in the world?"

"Yes." We nod then pad back to bed.

"Shocking," the smell of my mother.

Always the perfume comes gift-wrapped. My father makes the paper himself. He uses Scotch tape and as many hundred-dollar bills as it takes to get the job done.

Between the time Mae West shipped her mannequin to Schiaparelli and the time her costumes were ready, Miss West put on weight. Hollywood added "extenders" to the backs of her gowns.

Salvador Dalí

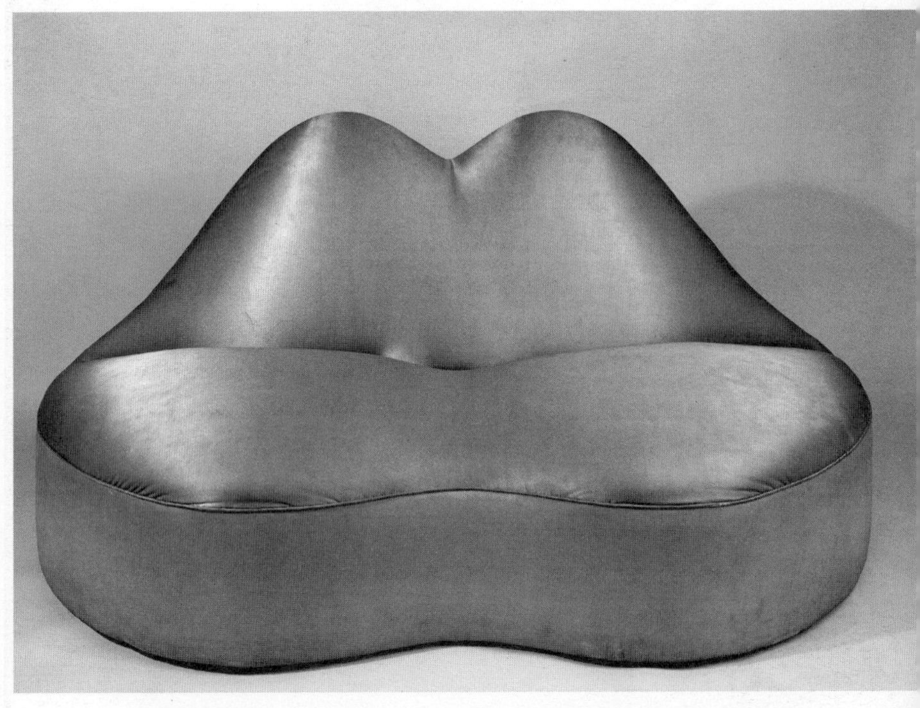

Three years later, Dalí and Jean-Michel Frank make Mae West's lips into a pink satin sofa for Schiaparelli's apartment. She turns it down. The Lip Sofa winds up in the ballroom/screening room of Baron Roland de l'Espée on the avenue Foch.

facing page: Salvador Dalí designs a living room furnished by Mae West's face. Her nose is the fireplace. Her lips are the sofa.

Three RAF airmen in their Mae West flotation vests (*left to right:* Flying Officer J. W. Simpson, Flight Lieutenant Peter W. Townsend, Pilot Officer H. C. Upton).

The first American ad for "Shocking" perfume. The bottle was designed by the artist Leonor Fini and based on the mannequin Mae West sent to Schiaparelli.

It takes thirty people to assemble a bottle of "Shocking." 1. Glass flowers (poppies, anemones, morning glories) handblown in Murano, Italy. 2. Two Murano green glass leaves. 3. Wires attached behind flowers and leaves. 4. Wires wrapped in green florist's tape. 5. Wires gathered like a nosegay and held in place by measuring tape. 6. Frosted-glass dauber. 7. Gilding on frosted-glass dauber. 8. Gilt cord wrapped around neck of dauber. 9. Membrane broken first time bottle is used. 10. Bottle made in France. 11. Silk-screened cotton tape measure. 12. Gold "navel" sticker. 13. "S" logo embossed on sticker. 14. Clear glass dome imported from Czechoslovakia. 15. White lace silk-screened on glass dome. 16. Pink velvet cushion for bottle. 17. Gold platform for pink cushion. 18. Pink velvet base for gold platform. 19. Perfume. 20. Close-up of glass morning glory with contrasting glass pistil.

chapter two

"The From Above"

Darling, can't you see I'm reading?

—*Audrey Volk*

My father's private library became my haven and my joy. I found, within the pages of rare and priceless books, a dream world of ancient religions and the worship of the arts.

—*Elsa Schiaparelli*

On a fat day he weighs 244. Everyone agrees he is big. When he was little he was big. At six feet one and a half inches, he fills the doorway. You hear him coming. He breaks Thanksgiving turkeys apart with his hands. He flips his 547-pound (wet weight) motorcycle onto its kickstand without rocking it. In his sculpture studio, he bends two-centimeter copper tubing without benefit of tools, pulling his lips back, clenching his teeth until the cords in his neck pop like the roots of a mangrove. And yet my father, Cecil Sussman Volk, proprietor of Morgen's West, tennis ace, fearsome racquetball opponent and former Southern Conference Wrestling Champion, reads books with the delicacy of a Victorian on a fainting couch. Propped by pillows, legs crossed at the ankle, he reads in bed, sighing, frowning, turning each page with gentle care, as if it were gold leaf. Anticipating the need to turn, sliding his right forefinger beneath the top corner, raising it a bit, then joining that finger through the paper with his thumb, he turns it, whipping his compact head to the next page. Always his pinky is raised.

Books are everywhere. Many are Modern Library Classics with a running torchbearer embossed on their spines. Many are books Audrey and Cecil read in college: *Tristram Shandy, Heart of Darkness, Madame Bovary, A Passage to India, War and Peace, Tender Is the Night, Remembrance of Things Past* (volume 1). They're stored in the living room in mahogany bookcases separated by a fake fireplace. Birch logs glow red in the chinks when a secret switch is flipped.

This is where Cecil hides his private library, behind the fake logs, the first place a child would look: *Tropic of Cancer* ("She had shaved it clean . . . not a speck of hair on it"), *Tropic of Capricorn* ("She's America on foot, winged and sexed"), *A Stone for Danny Fisher* ("I liked you, Danny, that's why"), *79 Park Avenue* ("Mister, some girls are born to be wives—but I was born for THIS!"), *Fanny Hill* (". . . and ascertaining the right opening, soon drove it up to the farthest"). There's a diet book for men, *The Fat Boy's Book* by Elmer Wheeler ("Run and hide from food that's fried. Cheer the host who serves a roast"), and a book of cartoons, *Over Sexteen.*

In the playroom, My Kingdom, the Greatest Room on

Earth, in addition to the wood-burning set, chemistry set, perfume-manufacturing kit, stamp album, art supplies and bug collection, there is the child-size house Cecil built, not a dollhouse but an actual child-scale one-room house with a front door and working doorbell, a red roof, real windows, a bed and an electric light. There is *The Book of Knowledge,* my mother's since childhood. Each volume is covered in flaking burgundy leather. Picking one up, your fingers turn red as if you've been eating pistachios. Finally there are what I think of as my books: the first 103 issues of the *Classics Illustrated,* great novels told in comic-book form crammed with twisty plots, history and lingo. Sometimes the material is so explosive it can't be contained. Instead of being split into black boxes, during dramatic peaks a full page is devoted to one frame. Getting home from school, I dive into them like Scrooge McDuck diving into his swimming pool of money. Some days I'm in the mood for *The Three Musketeers* ("En garde! Thrust home! You're dead!"). Some days the conniving torment of *Pudd'nhead Wilson* hits the spot ("De Lord have mercy on me, po' miserable sinner dat I is!"). *Moby-Dick* is good for being privy to a man's world and the lust for revenge. Ahab barks, "Avast, ye landlubber!" and "Stop!" can't hold a candle. I compare the way Jupiter in "The Gold-Bug" speaks to the way Uncle Tom speaks. "The Tell-Tale Heart," the dead man's heart thumping under the floorboards, terrifies. Worst is "The Murders on the Rue Morgue," a close-up of a crazed orangutan with human blood dripping off his fangs. Poe is read turning certain pages together.

My favorite *Classics Illustrated* is No. 42, *Swiss Family Robinson.* The Robinsons are like Polly Morgen, my New York grandmother. She knows how to "make do" too. When her children wanted candy, Nana caramelized sugar in a cast-iron skillet, poured it on waxed paper, then struck it with a hammer once it cooled. Old newspapers clean glass. She makes cookies out of leftover pie-crust dough and streusel out of leftover cookie. The Robinsons turn oyster shells into soup bowls. They lasso a giant sea turtle to power their raft. Thanks to *Swiss Family Robinson,* if my plane goes down en route to the Florida grandmother, I'll be fine on an island.

My mother doesn't buy books. She rents them. On Broadway, there's a bookstore called Womrath's. Best sellers spin on a metal rack. A new book rents at twenty-five cents for three days. If the book comes back late, each additional day there's a fifteen-cent penalty. Audrey prefers Womrath's to the local public library, the Saint Agnes Branch on Amsterdam Avenue. Books are free there, but she's got something against Amsterdam. "I don't care for Amsterdam Avenue," she has said more than once. "Or Columbus, for that matter." There's also a problem with the east side of Broadway. "The west side of Broadway is much better. It always has been. Even when I was little." If Audrey could redesign the Upper West Side of New York, it would go: Riverside Drive, West End Avenue, Central Park West. Those are the acceptable avenues, the avenues that meet desirable avenue criteria.

Between 3 and 6 p.m. every weekday, home from hostessing at Morgen's, Audrey reads in bed in her green velvet robe. She reads with her knees bent, the book propped against her thighs. Underneath her robe, she still wears the tube girdle and stockings she'd put on to dress for work. The bent-knee position allows her to "air out." She does not like to be disturbed when she reads. When interrupted, she makes a chilling gesture. She stabs her finger so hard into the sentence she's reading, you can hear it. She eyes you over the roof of the book and her look says, *This better be more important than what I'm reading.*

Audrey can finish a Womrath's book in less than three days. Once I can read, I read her books: *The Bad Seed, The Good Earth, Hiroshima, The Sea Around Us, Laughing Boy, Travels with My Aunt.* Once I've got the hang of reading, I'll read anything. I read the back of the Wheaties box at breakfast, ads on the bus, the NO SPITTING sign in English and Spanish on the subway. In the bathroom, I read what's written on the toothpaste. At the pedodontist's, the silver letters CRANE on his overhead lamp. I make words out of CRANE until Dr. Adelston is done: RAN, CAN, CANE, EAR, RACE, AN. CAR! CARE! ARE! ARC! CANER!!!

My mother's mother owns one book and says it is the only one she's ever loved. She keeps it mummified in Saran Wrap, locked in her silver closet. The title is *Fanny Kemble.* It has 387 pages and was written by Margaret Armstrong in 1938. Nana is convinced I'll like it. "It's the story of a beautiful actress from England who lives on a plantation in America, darling," she says.

I don't want to read her book. I don't want to read my sister's books either. Jo Ann is in thrall to series books with matching linen bindings: *The Bobbsey Twins, Cherry Ames—Student Nurse, Nancy Drew, Honey Bunch.* When she isn't beating me up or reading my diary, she swans around the apartment, clutching the latest one to her chest. I have zero interest in the books my friends are reading too, books about Joan of Arc, Florence Nightingale and Madame Curie. I want to read the books my mother reads. I want to know what is in those books that is better than spending time with me.

When Audrey finishes a Womrath's book, she leaves it on the bar in the foyer. Her books wait there like invitations: *Come. Trust me for a while. Let me take you for a ride.* That's where I find it, the book that arms me to separate. Years later, when I ask friends, "How old were you when you read your transformative book?" they say the same thing. They are prepubescent, ten or eleven. Twelve, the most. The magic age for the book that changes everything. Dr. Martin Bergmann, a psychoanalyst, tells me why this is so. Martin, the author of *The Anatomy of Loving* and *Understanding Dissidence and Controversy,* was analyzed by Edith Jacobson who was analyzed by Otto Fenichel who was analyzed by Sandor Rado who was analyzed by Karl Abraham who was part of Freud's Secret Committee. He is ninety-nine and has a busy practice. There's little about human behavior Dr. Martin Bergmann doesn't know.

He sits across from me on a plain wood chair. Two windows six feet tall frame the Central Park Reservoir. Asmalyks and Shekarlus, the kind of rugs Freud had, drape the furniture. Bookshelves tower floor to ceiling. It is a sunny, comfortable, unself-consciously beautiful room.

"I bet it makes your patients feel better just coming in here," I say.

"I know it makes me feel better."

He smiles and points to a black leather chair.

"Martin." I lean forward. "Do you remember what the first book you read was that changed your view of the world?"

He thinks. He rests his chin on his fist. Then he brightens: "It was *Kristin Lavransdatter* by Sigrid Undset."

"What was it about?"

"It was about a life in Norway. A young girl."

"What made it so special?"

"It opened to me the mystery of what women are like."

"How old were you when you read it?"

"Ten," Martin says. "No, eleven, I think."

So I say, "This is what I want to know, Martin: Why is it every person I ask, 'How old were you when you read the book that changed you?,' the answer is always ten or eleven? The answer is always prepuberty."

"But you have just answered the question yourself, Patricia."

"I have?"

"The book helps them into puberty. That is the time you begin to wonder whether the world is your family or there is an outside world. That is the age that marks the transition from the restricted world of childhood. Children are looking for an opportunity to know what the world is like and all the anxiety connected to it. It is the burden of every adolescent to worry about how they will fit into the world. Entering puberty, one is ready for a glimpse of the world beyond the home."

When Audrey finishes a book before it has to be returned, I read it. Some I put back on the bar after a chapter or two. Sometimes I'm puzzled by the book but keep reading anyway. Sometimes I don't get to the end before the three days are up. But there is one book I have to finish. I must. It can't go back to Womrath's before I get to the end. I say I have a sore throat and stay home from school. I hold the book in my hands and I'm shocked. The book that tells me everything I want to know, everything I need to know. This book is about someone who exasperates her mother. A girl who loves to draw. Who daydreams and does poorly in school. She writes poems and hatches plots. She likes being alone. Her older sister is the pretty one. She is loved by her parents but knows she's thought of as "difficult." She understands that if you can make someone laugh they can't stay angry with you. She knows that looking and imagining, that's where the real excitement is. There is a right way and a wrong way to do everything—how you sit, how you laugh, how you breathe—and she's not buying it. We have endless unacceptable traits in common, but she turns out okay. She does things my mother disdains, yet when she grows up she's a success. Which means I could do what my mother doesn't approve of and still be all right. The author is famous, but she's enough like my mother that she's familiar: She loves clothes. She works. She's a perfectionist. She's a terrible driver. She loves to walk. She loves to read. She's smart. She wishes she could sing. She doesn't mind being stared at and surrounds herself with people awed by her. She believes in doing what my mother calls "good works." She has a hair-trigger temper. She's opinionated and its handmaiden, bossy.

There's something else. Something more important, a magical thing that instantly frees: The woman who wrote the book calls herself "I," as if she is writing the book about herself, which, since it's an autobiography, she is. But then, in the next paragraph, she'll switch from "I" to calling herself "She." She calls herself "She" as if she is observing herself like a different person. At first this confuses. Then it makes sense: There is more than one way to see yourself. You can see yourself flat out and direct as "I." Or you can hover and look down at yourself from above, as if you are someone else. You can see yourself like your grandmother sees you or your mother. Or a teacher or a boy. Or a stranger. You can see yourself as if you've never met you before. "I" can also be "She." I'm ten and don't know the word "objectivity." I decide to call seeing yourself outside of yourself "The From Above." Using The From Above, you can see yourself from a distance. "I" becomes "She." The author uses The From Above when she brags, has something to confess or is miserable. I experiment with The From Above:

She was sure Eddie Fisher would love her if only they could meet.

She decided to glue the man's windshield wipers down because he stole her father's parking space.

Her mother still loved her even though she got a 20 on the math test.

Whoever you were, you were a different person to each person who knew you. How you saw yourself was a choice. The From Above let you see yourself through the eyes of anyone. You could see yourself a new way.

What do you do when you're little and know you can't be like your mother? I adore and am proud of my mother, but what she wants from me is blind adherence to the mystifying virtue of "seemly" behavior. Why must I sit with my ankles crossed? Why does she pinch my cheeks with rouge on her fingertips as I leave the apartment? Why are her parting words "Don't be loud!"? In a race with a boy, I have to let him win? Why does she care so much about how I look?

When I get home from a party, her first question is: "Were you the prettiest girl there?" Is there a way to answer that doesn't make you cringe?

You don't agree with what your mother thinks is important. You don't want to care what she thinks. At the very least, you'd rather care less. Your older sister tries to be like her. You watch. Over and over your sister fails.

You want to be you, whatever that is, not your mother's idea of you. You don't know what it takes, how much of it is luck. You suspect you're going to be all right in the world. You hope you are. You yearn for a signal. You're ripe for it. Sometimes it comes from a teacher. Or a relative. It could be a situation that shows you something about yourself you didn't know. Sometimes it's a book.

There is a coincidence. I have no idea what it means: My mother wears "Shocking" perfume by Elsa Schiaparelli. And the book that defuses her, the book that transforms me, is *Shocking Life* by Elsa Schiaparelli.

The From Above

Top row: Nana Polly and Poppy Herman, Uncle Bob and Aunt Barbara, "Aunt" Ruth. *Center row:* Eddie Fisher, "Aunt" Dorothy, "Aunt" Honey, Granny Ethel and Grandpa Jake. *Bottom row:* Jo Ann, Dad, Mattie, Mom, "Aunt" Horty.

The Schiaparelli logo, a woman made entirely of hearts, bore a startling resemblance to the logo on many of my parents' books. This had to mean something.

CLASSICS Illustrated
FEATURING STORIES BY THE WORLD'S GREATEST AUTHORS
No. 42
Swiss Family Robinson
15c in Canada and Foreign
By JONATHAN WYSS
H.C.KIEFER.

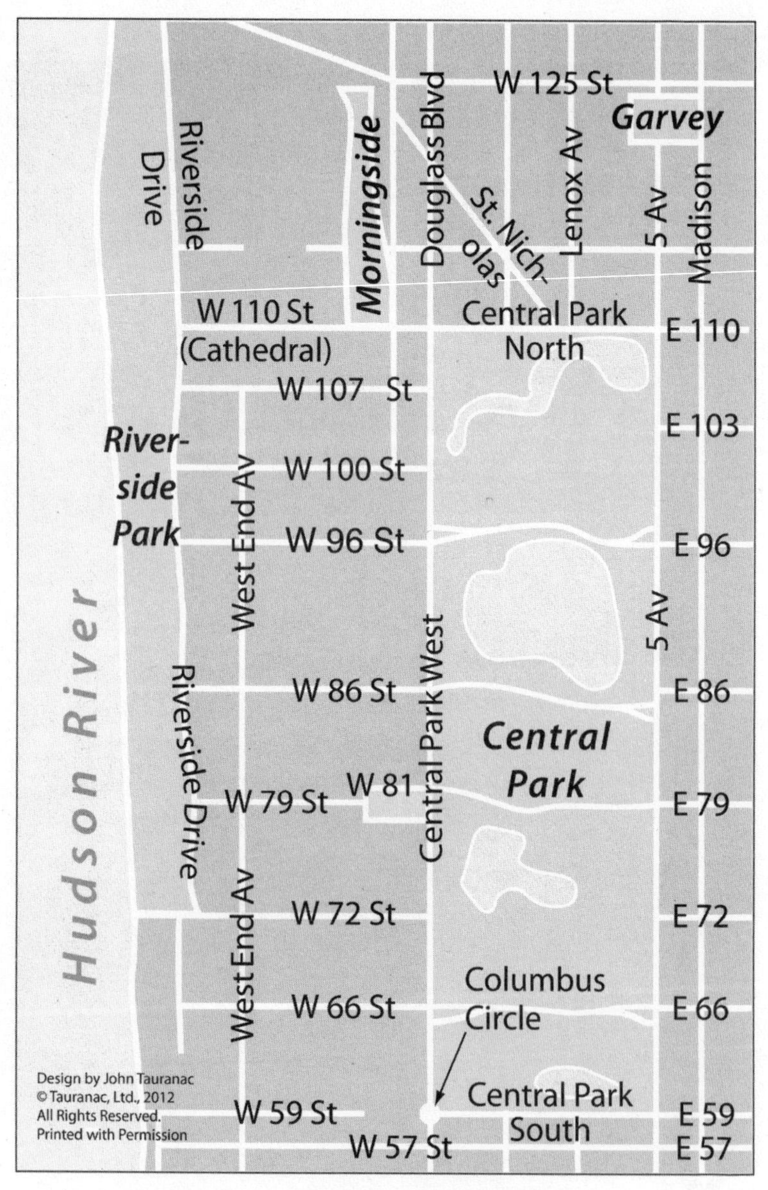

A map of the Upper West Side, minus Broadway, Columbus and Amsterdam.

chapter three

A Ring and a Mink

You only get to make a first impression once.

—*Audrey Volk*

I remember, when I was so small I could hardly read, seeing a drawing . . . of two men bathing on a solitary beach. They started to talk, got along splendidly, and after sunning themselves for a long time went behind different rocks to dress. One came out all smartness with a dangling lorgnette and a silver stick; the other in rags. Stupefied, they looked at each other, and with a cold nod each turned and went his separate way. They had nothing more to say to each other.

—*Elsa Schiaparelli*

We are in a restaurant. Two tables away, a man laughs. Audrey's swizzle stick stops.

"Born in Russia," she says. "Lives in Queens. Father a tailor."

All this from a laugh. From observing his clothes, his manner, and above all that merciless dead giveaway, his dentistry.

"You don't know that, Ma."

"Are you contradicting me?"

If she can tell everything about him, can he tell everything about us? Can anybody know about you from looking at you? Are we only as good as other people think we are? Is that why, when conversation flags in a restaurant, Audrey asks me to count so people at other tables will think we're engaged in lively repartee?

Audrey: "One, two, three!"

Me: "Four, five, six."

Audrey: "Seven. Eight. *Nine!*"

Me: "Ten! Ten! Ten!!!!"

Why does she care if strangers imagine we're living it up?

The first time you question your mother, you begin to suspect she could be fallible. I can't be like her. I don't want to be like her. Much of what she thinks is important, I don't. There has to be more than one way to be a woman. And if there is more than one way, chances are there are many.

I do like that my mother doesn't show off. Audrey is not materialistic. She has complete disdain for anyone wearing what she calls "Notice me!" clothes. But to go out in the world, to navigate the universe in a successful manner, to be recognized as a person of substance and treated as such, to be perceived as someone to be reckoned with, to optimize her chances in life, a woman needs a ring and a mink. All of Audrey's friends have a ring and a mink. Lunching at Schrafft's, they look like the Ring and Mink Club. Both grandmothers have a ring and a mink. The aunts too, though some rings are fake and some minks have mileage. Even so, all women in our family greet the day in a ring and a mink, properly geared for the vagaries of life.

Audrey's diamond is emerald-cut with two baguettes set in platinum. On the inside, it is hand-engraved with the day of her engagement and "CSV-AEM" in script. Like her beauty, the ring is classic. I love its icy punctuation of her manicured hand. Once a month my sister and I watch as she lovingly bathes it in hot water, Ivory and ammonia.

Her minks are made to order by our family furrier in the fur district on West Twenty-eighth Street. The family furrier is famous for being able to copy anything. You can bring Donald a Révillon ad and he copies the coat "line for line" at half what it goes for at Saks. The light in his showroom is ice blue. The couches are white damask, the wall-to-wall white plush. The place is freezing. The smell is dead animal. In what looks and feels like a fancy meat locker, Audrey trains her daughter in the art of pelt selection.

Lesson one: Female skins are better than male skins.

"They keep you just as warm as male skins but they weigh less," she instructs. "You can walk around all day in a department store in female skins without having to take your coat off and carry it."

Audrey tests the skins, flailing them above her head like semaphores. From that she can tell what the mink ate, its sex, general health, how old it was when it died and if it lived in the wild or spent its grim life cramped in a cage. Once she has culled enough happy healthy female pelts, she raises each one individually up to her lips. She closes in as if she is about to kiss the fur but at the last moment blows on it instead. Blowing bends the hairs. She's searching for a white one, one at least, proof the pelts are natural, not dyed. When she approves enough pelts to make a coat, Donald hooks them together on a metal ring that slips through holes where the mink's eyes were in better days. They hang there like a lucky hunter's bounty.

Once Donald gets the nod, there are at least three fittings. First, the canvas. Initially, a fur coat is cut in canvas, not fur. Audrey tries the canvas on, swirls in it, bends in it, crouches, walks fast, raises each arm individually as if hailing a cab, puts her fist on her hip, which forces the canvas to bunch behind her hand. She mimes every movement she could possibly make once the coat is cut in fur. The coat must have enough "swing" to cocoon me on windy days when we lockstep down Riverside Drive. Depending on the success of the canvas, how close it is to what my mother envisions, if all goes well, the next fitting will be in mink.

At the first actual mink fitting, Audrey has a million corrections. She poses on a white pedestal in front of a three-way mirror and confers with Donald, who works with a measuring tape around his neck and his sleeves rolled up. His assistant, a bent old man in a gray cotton jacket, wears a pincushion bracelet on his wrist.

Depending on how well this fitting goes, Audrey selects her lining from giant swatch books. She studies her button options, decides whether she wants buttons at all—as opposed to frogs, passementerie, or hidden closures—then checks the font book. She considers various type styles for her "AMV" monogram and picks the color of the thread. The monogram can be embroidered on the lining of the coat, or it can be hidden in the pocket for security. If someone steals your coat, thinking it's unmonogrammed, and you have to prove it's yours, you can turn the pocket inside out and say, "Aha!"

We are almost done. There is an interior-of-the-pocket discussion. Match the lining? Heavy satin? Velvet? It is a family tradition, when you are paying a lot for something—when you are paying cold cash as restaurant families do—to ask for a "gift." Will a mink scarf be included in the price?

In the best of all possible worlds, if everything is perfect, the third fitting is the last. But it never is. Another half-inch off the hem? A deeper cuff? An extra hook on the collar so it "frames" the face like a ruff? Audrey instructs Donald. Donald instructs the old man. Everyone in the showroom tells me how beautiful my mother is, how stunning she looks in her coat. They pat my head and say, "Someday, little girl, someday you will have a mink coat too." In a glass bowl in the center of a coffee table, Donald keeps the candy of choice in places where children wait for mothers. Each butterscotch disk comes wrapped in murky yellow cellophane for daughters learning how to buy a mink.

Elsa Schiaparelli has a mink too. She also has a ponyskin, opossum, antelope, black monkey, colobus monkey, nutria, civet, ermine, jaguar, chinchilla, rabbit, rooster feather, leopard and the occasional seal. She trims lingerie and bathing suits with mink and dyes fox to look like tortoiseshell. A favorite fur is Russian broadtail (fetal lambs with flat coiled hair also known as Swakara or Astrakhan or Karakul). Her bowling shoes are covered in ocelot. She wears a hat made out of the taxidermied face of a cheetah with jewels for eyes. She wears it with the cat's nose centered over hers so her face is in his open mouth, as if Elsa Schiaparelli has been swallowed feet-first.

She doesn't wear a ring in Audrey's sense of the word. If she had an engagement ring, she got rid of it when she divorced her only husband, Count Wilhelm de Wendt de Kerlor. Instead, she invents a three-part diamond pinky ring, the last joint covering the fingertip like a thimble.

Some of her jewelry is real, some of it is "paste." She likes big jewelry, lots of it. Pearls, up to four strands, a gold-and-emerald bib, an armload of her favorite chunky bracelets, clips. She invents a giant rhinestone she calls the Aurora Borealis. Depending on how light hits it, deep facets turn blue, green or Shocking Pink and sometimes all three at once. She sets them in gold or silver and makes them into bracelets, earrings and extraordinarily beautiful necklaces that vary from simple to wildly baroque. She mixes real with fake, making no distinction between the beauty of both.

Audrey does not approve of costume jewelry. She wears a diamond circle pin my father gave her and a watch with a leather strap. When she goes out in the evening, she takes her Lucien Piccard watch with its pearl, ruby and sapphire bracelet out of the vault. She will lend it to me one night for a blind date at the Playboy Club with Barry Goldwater's nephew. I will forget it on the sink in the ladies' room when I wash my hands and she will shake her head, nothing more, when I tell her. "That Patty," I hear her laughing on the phone. "I'm thrilled she hasn't lost her nose."

Someday comes. When I graduate from college Audrey says, "It's time for a mink." She takes me to Donald. Again I get to study how to flail and blow on fur. At the second fitting, when it's time to pick the monogram, I opt for a classic script and ask Donald to have it read:

For Patty
Love, Mom

Donald does it wrong. The monogram reads:

To Patty
Love, Mom

but although there is a world of difference between "For" and "To," "To" being a dedication so it makes no sense and "For" being a gift, I don't make a fuss.

I feel like a Valkyrie in my mink, or like Moondog, like I should be standing on Sixth Avenue with a spear. But when it's pricking cold in New York, when the wind bites like needles, I'm grateful. My mother is still keeping me warm. Audrey never gives something to one daughter without giving it to the other so my sister has a mink too. She wears hers less than I do. Jo Ann lives in Coral Gables.

Schiaparelli in the jaws of a cheetah.

Schiaparelli asked Meret Oppenheim to make her a bracelet out of fur. When Picasso saw it he said, "One can make anything out of fur!" Oppenheim then created *Object* using Chinese gazelle. André Breton renamed it *Le Déjeuner en fourrure* after Manet's *Le Déjeuner sur l'herbe.*

Elsa Schiaparelli wore these to bowl.

Schiaparelli, in a box jacket and matching hat of civet, arriving in New York at the onset of World War II.

My New York grandmother, Polly Morgen, in a
mink and matching toque à la Schiaparelli.

Audrey, in a big mink, takes her girls to Rockefeller Center.

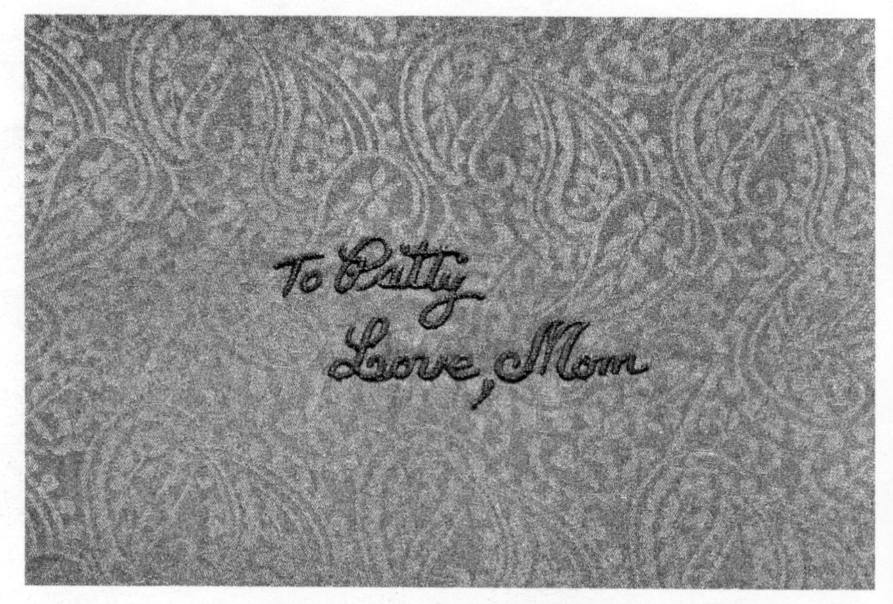

The monogram on the coat my mother bought me.
It was supposed to read "For Patty," not "To Patty."

Louis Thomas Hardin, aka "Moondog," was a blind American composer, poet and inventor of musical instruments. He hung out on West Fifty-sixth Street wearing his interpretation of the Norse God Odin. Moondog's music influenced Philip Glass and Steve Reich. Three albums and fifty singles are available on iTunes.

chapter four

Something in Common

I have never quite understood my father's relations with my mother or how they happened to have two children in ten years.

—*Elsa Schiaparelli*

Nobody needs to know how old you are. It's nobody's beeswax.

—*Audrey Volk*

Where she was born isn't there anymore. West 179th Street was razed sixty years ago. There's no trekking uptown to pay homage to the site. Where Audrey Elaine Volk (née Morgen) was born there's a two-story twelve-lane highway. It links the George Washington Bridge via the Henry Hudson Parkway to I-95 and points east. Less than a mile long, the Trans-Manhattan Expressway bisects the borough at its narrowest point. A bus terminal was built on top of the highway. Then four high-rises on top of the bus terminal. West 179th Street isn't a street. But that's where, at the height of Washington Heights, the highest point in the city, 265 feet above sea level, she is born—my mother—at home, in a two-bedroom apartment in a four-story building on a death-defying hill famous for breakneck sledding, hare-brained bicycle stunts, roller-skating daredevils, boxcar certifiables and tragic black-ice tailspins culminating in the frozen estuary of the Hudson. My mother is born there on that steep street at home in her mother's bedroom. Assisted by a local doctor, Polly Ann Morgen (née Lieban) gives birth to her second child. In attendance are her sisters, Gertie and Ruthie, who drape white sheets from the ceiling to sterilize the room.

Her husband doesn't want this baby.

"I need you in the store," Herman says.

This is true. Polly works magic at Morgen's Cafe. Customers love her. She makes them feel welcome. She's primed to like you. If she doesn't know your name, it's "darling." Her face lights up when you breeze through the door. Not so Herman Morgen, cool appraiser of human foibles. He sees right through you. He's got your number, whether you have a number or not.

"Would I lie to you, Polly?"

Is he asking her to "fall" down the stairs? Not the Hanger Man again. What if this time he punctures her bladder? Mildred's has to be professionally emptied twice a week. What if she got an infection like Ida?

"With God as my witness, the last thing we need is another Bobby," Herman says.

Bobby. He gets into fistfights with boys who wear eyeglasses. He shows up at assembly in a fake mustache. He mows down old Mr. Rosenheim in the hallway with his bicycle and gets suspended from school for putting a dead mouse in his teacher's lunch bag. Polly has to bribe the principal with turkey sandwiches not to banish him from school. If you told Bobby the pudding had to cool first, he burned his tongue. Coming home from the restaurant, Herman is greeted with a litany—Bobby crashed into the end table and broke your sister's vase, Bobby threw his Brussels sprouts out the window, Bobby rode the back of the ice truck. Herman explodes. He whips off his belt. Polly cries while Bobby's beaten. Then the next day, the cycle repeats: Polly tattles, Herman whips, Polly weeps. But she loves her boy. She doesn't want him to be an only child. She's one of five.

"Darling, you don't want Bobby to have a brother or sister? You want him to be all alone in the world?"

She's too smart to disagree with her husband flat-out. "Bobby is in school until three every day," she continues. "Velma is here with nothing to do. She can watch the baby. I'll be back in the store before you know it."

"You don't have to go to the Hanger Man," Herman says. "Faye knows a real doctor in Washington."

Was there a time when Herman Morgen was softer? Postcards secretly passed to Polly before they were married are filled with tenderness. One from 1917 is prophetic. The top half shows a beautiful young couple kissing, backlit by the moon. The bottom half shows them in bed, newly ugly, with a squawking baby between them. Printed on the top it says, "Nothing shall ever come between us." And on the back Herman wrote: "Dear Polly, Lets trust to god nothing shall come between us in many a moon. Love and kisses from Herman." It was said he sank in a chair and cried when a telegram arrived saying his mother, Anna, had died.

On an icy morning in January, Herman leaves for work. When he comes home in the evening, Polly is swaddling a newborn.

"It's a girl, darling." She folds back the receiving blanket. "Did you ever?"

She places the baby in his arms. He looks at his daughter. Her beauty astonishes him. "Never."

"Never?"

"Never!"

He has a daughter, a beautiful daughter, a beautiful perfect daughter, perfect beyond anything he could have imagined, perfectly round, perfectly symmetrical, with golden curls and fat cheeks. And she's his, the most beautiful baby girl in the world.

"Do you like the name 'Audrey,' darling?" Polly says. "After your mother?"

Herman throws on his overcoat and races to Broadway.

"I'll take everything," he tells the florist.

Their room is transformed into an arbor. At the foot of the bed, Herman kneels and clasps his hands: "Forgive me, please God, for not wanting my Audrey."

From that day on Audrey is the prettiest and the smartest. If she gets below an A on a test, the teacher is anti-Semitic. If she loses the spelling bee, the winner's word was easier. Bobby's wife would later explain: "When Audrey was born, Herman wouldn't let go of her because of what he had said. Your grandfather worshipped Audrey."

Elsa Schiaparelli is born at home too. But unlike the Morgens, the Schiaparellis are aristocrats. They can trace their lineage back to Napoleon. Celestino Schiaparelli is a friend of King Victor Emmanuel II. Both of them are serious collectors of ancient gold coins and they trade.

An Egyptologist and expert in Sanskrit and Persian, Professore Schiaparelli is appointed by the king to head the Lincei Library, in the Palazzo Corsini, a masterpiece of Renaissance architecture in Rome. It is 1875. The position comes with a sprawling family apartment right there, where four hundred years earlier Michelangelo was a dinner guest.

Celestino consults his personal library to find the perfect name for a son. He pores over illuminated manuscripts—Homer, Aesop, the Books of Saints, Pizarro's conquests, Scheherazade, the medieval Book of Hours, the Zodiac, Arab poets, priceless Sanskrit texts. He consults the Koran and the Thousand and One Nights. Signora Maria Luisa Schiaparelli is expecting again. His exquisite daughter, Beatrice, is ten years old. Professore Schiaparelli is certain this time it will be a boy.

The baby arrives on September 10, 1890. It is a girl.

Ten days later, the Schiaparellis traverse the Via della Lungara and walk north along the Tiber toward Saint Peter's. After fifteen minutes, they make a left and begin the cobblestone approach to the basilica. Beautiful Beatrice, who is said to resemble the Vatican's Pallas Athena, keeps pace beside the sturdy German wet nurse cradling her new sister. Together the family climbs the steps of the cathedral. They proceed through the center door, passing the Pontifical Swiss Guards rigid in their red, yellow and blue uniforms and armed with rapiers and flamberges.

A priest waits by the baptismal font. Halfway up the left aisle, the Schiaparellis pause by what remains of the bronze foot on the statue of Saint Peter. The toes have worn off from countless kisses.

"Io ti battenzo . . ." The priest begins the service. Suddenly he stops. *"Mi scusi,"* he says. *"A proposito, qual'è il nome della bambina?"*

Maria Luisa and Celestino look at each other. No one has thought to find a name for a girl.

There is an awkward silence. The wet nurse steps forward: "Elsa," she says, naming the baby after herself.

The baby is christened Elsa Luisa Maria Schiaparelli. It is a name Elsa Schiaparelli loathes. She will call being named Elsa her "first disappointment." She will insist everyone—her daughter, her grandchildren, friends, clients, her employees, her lovers—call her "Schiap."

Audrey and Cecil are expecting their second child to be a boy too. They don't have a name for me either.

"Victoria," Cecil says. "Victoria Volk."

"Patricia," Audrey counters from her hospital bed. "Patricia Gay Volk."

"Victoria," Cecil persists. "Vicki Volk."

Audrey is exhausted. She sinks back into her pillows. "Name her anything you want, Cecil. Name her Mary Jane for all I care."

He does.

I'm twelve when I come across the first birth certificate in a box in a storage closet. It reads Mary Jane Volk and she was born on my birthday. I find it the year Elvis Presley records Carl Perkins's hit "Blue Suede Shoes." My mother laughs but I'm convinced. Like Elvis, I have a dead twin.

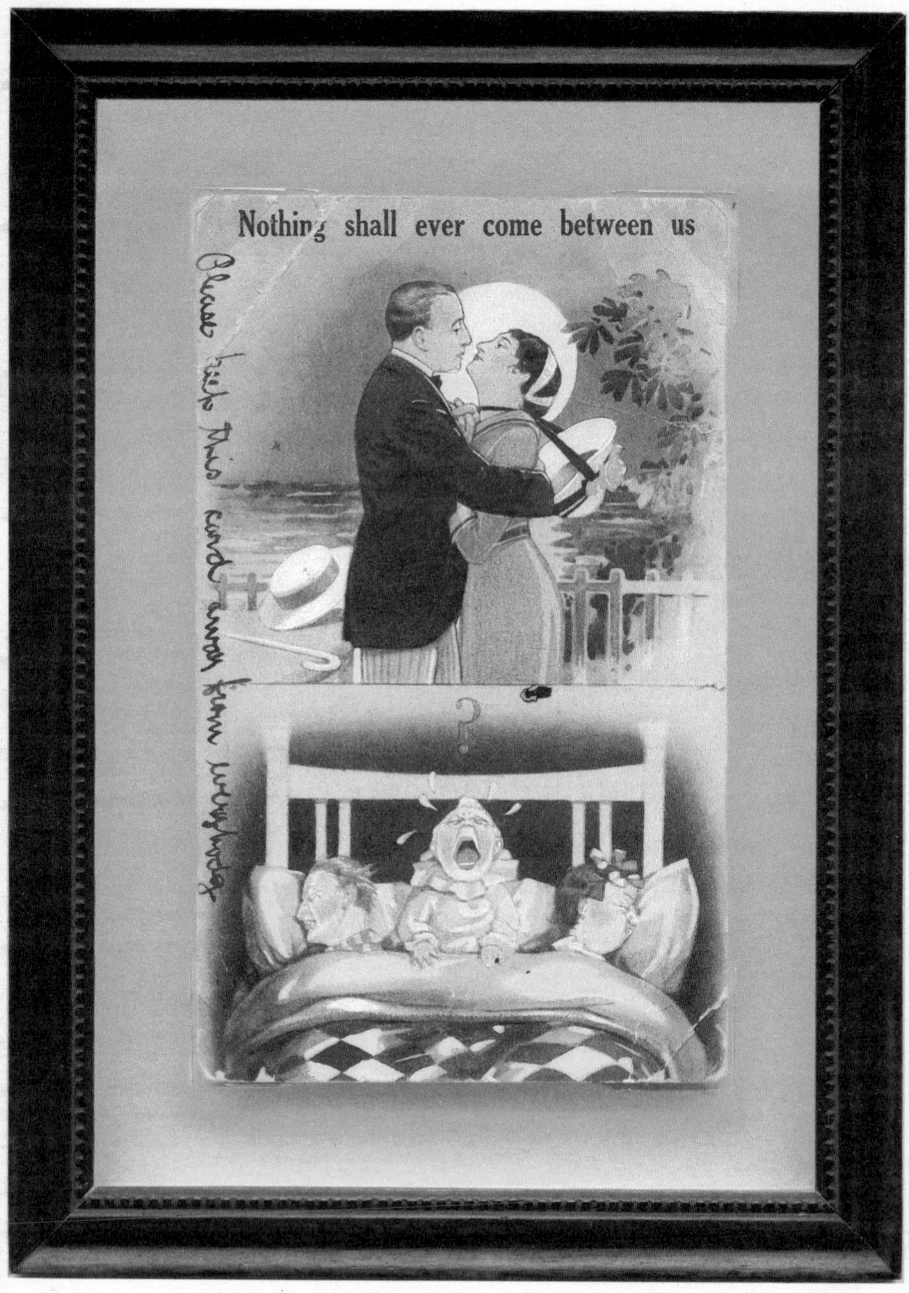

Visionary postcard Herman Morgen gave to his fiancée.

Statue of the Pallas Athena, aka *Athena,* in the Vatican.

previous page: The Palazzo Corsini, home of the Lincei Library and birthplace of Elsa Maria Luisa Schiaparelli.

The statue of St. Peter in the Vatican and his foot, worn smooth from countless kisses.

DEPARTMENT OF HEALTH
CITY OF NEW YORK

Certificate of Birth Registration

THIS IS TO CERTIFY *that the following extract has been taken from a record of birth registered with the Bureau of Records in the Borough where the birth occurred.*

Name Mary Jane Volk

Sex Fem. *Date of Birth* July 16" 1943 *Number* 23878

Place of Birth Polyclinic Hosp. *Borough* Man.

Mayor — *Registrar of Records* — *Commissioner of Health*

110 River Dr.

85 H-1939-2

First birth certificate.

cc vm

Department of Health **City of New York**

BUREAU OF VITAL RECORDS AND STATISTICS

Certification of Birth

THIS IS TO CERTIFY *that according to Birth Record No.* 23878 *filed in the* Manhattan *Office of this Bureau on* July 20, 1943

Patricia Gay Volk

Sex female *was Born in the City of New York, on* July 16, 1943

In witness whereof, the seal of the Department of Health of the City of New York has been affixed hereto this 23rd *day of* August 1943

C. W. Lynn, M.D.
Assistant Registrar of Records

Ernest L. Stebbins M.D.
Commissioner of Health

Registrar of Records

By Vehanoush May

Warning: This certification is not valid if it has been altered in any way whatsoever or if it does not bear the raised seal of the Department of Health.

324 84H-50M-82542

Second birth certificate.

chapter five

Gambling

Taking a risk without anticipating the consequences? Grandiose. There's no other word for it.

—*Audrey Volk*

She was to continue to gamble all her life but never again on the gaming tables.

—*Elsa Schiaparelli*

Audrey does not gamble. Make that, she doesn't take chances. In other words, given a choice, my mother is 110 percent risk-averse. She gambles only when she can completely without a doubt control both the circumstances and the outcome, specifically, any possible downside, so that definitionally speaking the risk isn't risky and she's not in fact gambling. Audrey does not like to lose. She does not lose unless losing spawns an advantage. On occasion, when she does lose, the extent of her loss is predetermined.

This means she takes chances by creating a situation where she doesn't mind losing if she does. She loses *voluntarily.* In such a case the risk is justified.

Financially, Audrey has a reputation for being "good with money." She fans it. She whispers to it and blows on it. Every weekday when *The New York Times* lands on our doormat she ignores the front page and heads straight for the microscopic stock-market columns. She has a system: When a stock doubles, she sells half and reinvests the profit in a new stock. Her system is conjoined to free tips from a wealthy friend who is a client of the most revered portfolio-manager in New York. Audrey keeps no more than 25 percent of her assets in the market. It's burned into her brain: Herman Morgen was okay during the Great Depression because he was not in the stock market. Overnight her father was a rich man by virtue of not having lost a penny.

This does not mean Audrey is averse to spending. She spends but she discriminates. She relishes "good value," getting something for her money. So it's puzzling what she does on vacations:

Every winter, Audrey and Cecil take a ten-day holiday someplace hot. Along with Mattie Sylvia Lee Myles Weems Watts, our beloved housekeeper, our New York grandparents move into the apartment to watch us. This presents an annual revelation in what you can get away with:

"Mom always lets me stay up for *Lux Video Theatre.*"

"We always get seconds on dessert."

"I'm allowed to wear my party dress to school."

On the downside, daily bowel reports are mandatory:

"Yes, Nana. After breakfast. Two."

"Were they hard or soft, *zezakeppeleh*?"

Thumbprint cookies and Barton's Chocolate Kisses are on tap. But if you ask for a glass of water, Polly worries you have diabetes. If you scrape your knee roller-skating, she's on lockjaw alert. We teeter on the brink of catastrophe. Every stomachache could be appendicitis. On the other hand, all you have to do is say, "I forgot to study for the test," and Polly lets you stay home from school. She'll take you to the playground and you'll have it to yourself.

Then one day Audrey bursts through the front door, tan as caramel, more beautiful than ever, arms loaded with presents. She tosses her mink on the bed, the quicker to hug us. We unwrap our coconut-head piggy banks from San Juan, or sombreros from Acapulco, or turquoise clamper bracelets from Arizona. We model grass skirts from Maui or bambouches from Marrakech and from Las Vegas something we've never seen before, a one-piece dress with a pleated skirt that is actually shorts, a skort! Fringed leather jackets! Beaded belts! Marimbas and tomahawks! How happy she is to see us! So many presents you could almost forget how much you'd missed her, her touch, her smell. So many presents her bed is a nest of crunchy cellophane excelsior.

Then I overhear a conversation:

"How did you do, darling?" Polly asks.

"The first night, I was up eighty. The second night, I was down fifty. The third night I lost everything. The next night, I broke even. All told, I came in about twenty ahead, Mother."

Later I screw up the courage to ask, "Are you a gambler, Ma?"

She laughs at my concern. "Every night," she explains, "when your father and I are on vacation, before we go to bed, I slip down to the casino. But I'm very, very careful, darling. I never bring more than a fixed amount with me. I never bring a penny more than I can afford to lose."

"How much?"

"Fifteen dollars," she says. "I consider that not too much to pay for an evening's entertainment. If I lose it all, if I lose every single cent, all I've spent is what two theater tickets cost and I've had a marvelous time. And if I win, well then there's extra money I wasn't even counting on."

"But Ma! That's gambling!"

"Technically speaking, Patty, yes. But I always come out ahead, even if I lose my fifteen dollars, *because I've been amused.* I've had a good time. Only instead of seeing *Where's Charlie?* or *Oklahoma,* I've had my evening's entertainment in a casino." Then she adds, "Did you know, darling, while you're gambling, they bring you free food and anything you want to drink?"

We are a restaurant family. I know which end is up. "Don't they lose money?"

"No," she says, then adds a favorite phrase: " 'It's good business.' "

"Why?"

"They want you to stay at the table. They don't want you to leave because you're thirsty or hungry. They want you to stay there so you can keep losing money."

God, I think, *my mother is brilliant.*

Schiap is brilliant too but she takes chances. She tries things without knowing in advance they'll succeed. "Reckless," Audrey would call her. Schiap plunges in and pays for it. She strikes me as fearless. Her life feels like a high-wire act but instead of scaring me, it exhilarates. She is six when she learns Jesus walked on water. Fully dressed, she leaps into a swimming pool. It's filled with quicklime. At seven, she comes across a book in her father's library with Leonardo's engravings of his inventions. She's dazzled by his flying machines, especially the ornithopters, wings laced to your arms. You leap off a cliff then flap them like a bat. She climbs to the second floor of the Palazzo Corsini, opens an umbrella and jumps, landing in a heap of manure. When she's fourteen, a book of her poetry is published. She's betting her father won't see it. For a young woman of her station, exposing her erotic fantasies is scandalous. But *Arethusa* is widely reviewed and her parents ship her off to a convent. She goes on a hunger strike. Celestino brings her home. In Nice during the Great War, she puts on her best dress and heads for Monte Carlo. She walks past the Hôtel de Paris, enters the glittery casino and slips onto a seat at the roulette wheel. It doesn't take long to grip how bad the odds are. She moves to trente-et-quarante, then finally tries her luck at baccarat. She loses everything. The casino freights her home. On a string around her neck so the conductor can't miss it, a railway voucher reads: "With the compliments of the casino."

At twenty-three, to learn English, Schiap accepts a job at an orphanage on the outskirts of London. On her day off, on a whim, she buys a ticket for a lecture on theosophy. She takes a seat in the auditorium. The lights dim. A young man of Polish-Swiss-French descent, a slender man with deep-set eyes and blond hair, strides onto the stage in a cutaway. He grabs both sides of the podium and glares at the audience. Schiap falls in love with Count Wilhelm de Wendt de Kerlor on the spot.

Thirteen years later, she is the daredevil darling of couture. One of her friends, Jeanne Lanvin, heads the Syndicat de la Couture. She invites Schiaparelli to participate in the 1937 Exposition Internationale des Arts et Techniques dans la Vie Moderne. Countries from all over the world set up pavilions along the Seine. Schiap bursts with ideas. Then she reads the rules. Lanvin's parameters are *pointilleux.* You can't do this, you can't do that. One restriction states all couturiers must use the same mannequin, a faceless, fat-hipped terra-cotta giantess seven feet tall. To re-create the floaty sylph of Schiap's new Butterfly Dress, it could never be right. Her latest collection will look terrible on what she refers to as "that dreary mannequin."

Schiap protests.

"It's up to you," Lanvin tells her. "*Le choix, c'est le vôtre.* You can obey the rules like everyone else or you can not participate."

Yes, all right, she will use *le monstre.* She will obey the rules. But she will do it the Schiaparelli way. What hasn't been thought of can't be prohibited. Schiap takes a chance. She lays turf on the floor of her exhibition space, making it look out of doors. Then she subverts the purpose of a mannequin. Instead of dressing it, she lays the mannequin flat on its back. The mannequin is naked, *en plein air,* her legs spread outward. Schiap tucks flowers around the behemoth and stretches a wash line above it from two stylized trees. Using clothespins, she hangs "all the clothes of a smart woman, even to panties, stockings and shoes." She hasn't broken a single rule.

Her exhibit makes headlines. A gendarme is posted to keep order. The fashion magazines unite and refuse to print pictures of what they call the naked corpse. A gentleman leaves a condolence card by its derrière. Schiap rights the mannequin to a sitting position. Even so, it infuriates. Lanvin's restrictions spark the one exhibit crowds line up to see.

Does Marcel Duchamp visit his good friend's tableau?

Last year, in Philadelphia to see the Duchamps, I realize Schiap's spread-eagle *plein-air* nude may have been the inspiration for his spread-eagle *plein-air* nude in *Étant donnés: 1° La Chute d'eau/2° Le Gaz d'éclairage* ("Given: 1. The Waterfall 2. The Illuminating Gas). This is not noted in Calvin Tomkins's encyclopedic *Duchamp: A Biography.* Duchamp began working on *Étant donnés* in 1946, nine years after the *Exposition internationale. Étant donnés* occupied him for the next twenty years. It became his final work of art. Jasper Johns calls *Étant donnés* "the strangest work of art any museum has ever had in it." It resides now, permanently, in the exact spot Duchamp chose for it. You enter a small, unlit, windowless room. Set into the wall on your left is an ancient wooden door Duchamp found, after years of searching, in a small Spanish village not far from Cadaqués. The door is faded and splintered. It opens in the center. Only it never opens. If you want to know what is behind the door, you must look through two peepholes drilled into it. Then, surrounded by pitch black, floating in limbo, you will see a brick wall. In the center of the wall, there is an irregular hole. Bricks are missing as if an explosion blew them out. Through this hole, you see a woman lying on her back in the woods. She is naked, *en plein air,* her legs spread outward. Duchamp's *femme au naturel* is holding a Bec Auer gas lamp, similar to the first one Duchamp drew when he was eleven. She has no hair on her body. (Duchamp detested female body hair. He asked his women to shave.) The cleft of her vagina is front and center but it doesn't look like a vagina. It looks like skin that's been slashed. No matter how you try, no matter how you shift your body or your eyes, you can't see one twig more than Duchamp wanted you to see. "Why don't artists require people to look at a painting from a specified distance?" he asked John Cage. There is no choice when viewing *Étant donnés.* You are physically forced to see it precisely the way Duchamp wanted you to. Is she dead? Was she raped? *Étant donnés* speaks to a universal anxiety: coming upon a naked body in nature. As a little girl I was mesmerized by pictures of Manet's *Déjeuner sur l'herbe.* It's a beautiful day. Two men are enjoying a picnic in the woods. They don't seem to notice they are in the company of a completely naked woman. In the distance, another naked woman bathes in a glen. (I used to think these two naked women were the same person, that because the woman in the background was softly focused, I was seeing the past as well as the present.)

In *Étant donnés,* the woman's skin is lovely and real-looking. First Duchamp tried tinting parchment. Then he tried leather. He found what he wanted in pigskin. Translucent, painted on the side making contact with the plaster, pigskin worked. His nicknames for the *corps,* which is cast from the torso of a lover, Maria Martins, and the left hand of his final wife, Alexina "Teeny" Matisse, were "*ma femme au chat ouvert*" ("my woman with the open pussy") and his playful, irreverent "*N.D.* (*Notre Dame*) *des désirs*" ("Our Lady of Desires"). In his *Manual of Instructions* for reassembling *Étant donnés* when it was shipped to Philadelphia, Duchamp refers to her as "*le nu.*"

Here's the thing. It's pure Duchamp. I laughed when it hit me: If you blacken the background of *Étant donnés* then turn that image on its side, the negative space between her arms and legs forms two letters. Reading left to right, they are "M" and "D."

Schiap's naked spread-eagled mannequin caused a riot at the Paris Exhibition of 1937.

The door Duchamp found near Cadaqués.
He drilled two peepholes into it.

Étant donnés: 1° La Chute d'eau/2° Le Gaz d'eclairage. Jasper Johns called it "the strangest work of art any museum has ever had in it."

If you black out the background to *Étant donnés,* then turn it on its side, the negative space forms the letters "M" and "D."

Le Déjeuner sur l'herbe.

chapter six

Manner of Dress

Just because it looks good on a model in a magazine, doesn't mean it will look good on you. Know what works.

—Audrey Volk

Women dress alike all over the world: They dress to be annoying to other women.

—Elsa Schiaparelli

Her look can be summed up in a word: Crisp. She lives ruffle- and flounce-free. Nothing dangles or blows in the breeze. She wakes up with perfect hair. The click of her red fingernails against the piano keys, the whish-whoosh of her stockings, the stutter of her heels in the hallway—kuh-luh-KLICK, kuh-lah-KLACK—broadcast crisp. She is streamlined by the Art Deco definition—passing through water, she would cause the least disturbance. Her crispness is abetted by a God-given asset, stick-straight hair.

Curlies can't be crisp no matter what. When she tosses her head, her hair moves of a piece, a waterfall of hair, what the French call *en cascade*.

For daywear, Audrey prefers sculptural clothes that elucidate her form, pencil skirts with kick pleats or slits so she can taper mermaid-svelte yet walk with a long stride, walk crisp. When she wears a sweater with a skirt, she wears it the Audrey way, tucked in tight, emphasizing her toned tidiness. The sweater is disciplined by a leather belt that sports an unusual buckle—a lion's head, say, or a crown—drawing attention to her waist. Above all, she is what she calls "buttoned up," edited to the bone, neatest of the neat, cleanest of the clean, clean being a major component of crisp. She radiates high-polished meticulosity. Earrings are taboo ("Only gypsies pierce their ears"), and anything "frou-frou," although she is not above wearing a Bill Blass scarlet felt carnation if it comes on a taupe Bill Blass suit. But as wondrous as her clothes are, as fine as she looks in them, they take a back seat to her face. Clothes can't compete. Her face is the star. This is clear early on. By the time she's sixteen, her look has gelled. She dresses differently from other coeds. Simply draped evening gowns are Railway Expressed from Russeks, silk shirts and bomber cardigans from Bonwit Teller. She stores her angora sweaters in the Sigma Delta Tau freezer so they won't fluff off. "Park Avenue Audrey," her sorority sisters call her. Her home is at 845 West End Avenue, but she's Park Avenue crisp.

As a married lady, working in the family restaurant, she shifts to designer clothes. Because Morgen's is in the garment center, she's on a first-name basis with the best "houses." She can "get up" to showrooms. Shopping at Bergdorf's, when she falls in love with a Geoffrey Beene, she checks the tag and jots the style number down. At home, she dials the manufacturer:

"It's Audrey from Morgen's, darling," she says. "You wouldn't happen to have T6136J in navy in an eight, would you?"

If they have it—"*How marvelous, darling!*"—they sell it to her wholesale. It's good business dressing Audrey. All the top designers, manufacturers and buyers wait behind her red velvet rope. They have nothing else to look at till they're seated. She's a walking advertisement for Larry Aldrich, Gino Paoli, Claire McCardell, Pauline Trigère, Teal Traina, and her three "B"s: Brooks, Blass and Beene. She looks terrific in their clothes. She shops at Loehmann's on Fordham Road too, where you can find couture (once the miracle of a black Lurex Norell for eight dollars) at the deepest of the steepest deep discounts. What pleasure is there in spending fifteen hundred dollars for a Norell? That takes money, not brains. But to wear a Norman Norell you have essentially stolen, that is a coup. Her favorite saleslady, Miss Sylvia, hides an 8 she suspects Audrey will like in the 14 rack, then gives Mom a call.

On occasion, a manufacturer asks to "borrow" one of Audrey's Loehmann's finds so he can copy it. Once, when a favorite Cardin is returned to her, it doesn't fit right. It has been dissected by a pattern-maker, then resewn by someone careless. Audrey says nothing to the manufacturer. He is a customer. She doesn't wear the dress again.

She has the right clothes for specific events. A fitted black suit and veiled hat for funerals. In the summer, a white piqué halter top for picnics. Hacking jackets, knife-edge slacks and tailored shirts for the weekends. Cashmere polos. Structured dinner suits and sweeping ball gowns. Her jodhpurs have little cuffs to protect the horse from the buckles on her riding boots. Her tennis dresses are so white they glow. After a game on clay courts, Cecil cleans her sneakers with Clorox on a toothbrush.

She believes in quality, not quantity. A woman should have twenty-four upholstered hangers in her closet and love each item hanging on them. When she gets a new blouse, an old blouse goes. Audrey believes in Laver's Law. It is a fashion timetable developed by James Laver, playwright, bon vivant and a curator at the Victoria & Albert Museum. Mr. Laver explicates the life cycle of a dress:

Indecent—10 years before its time
Shameless—5 years before its time
Daring—1 year before its time
Smart—Current fashion
Dowdy—1 year after its time
Hideous—10 years after its time
Ridiculous—20 years after its time
Amusing—30 years after its time
Quaint—50 years after its time
Charming—70 years after its time
Romantic—100 years after its time
Beautiful—150 years after its time

Schiap is Indecent. Audrey is Smart. Her closet turns over yearly. My sister and I are built differently. Jo's long-waisted and has broad shoulders. I have a tiny waist and Gaston Lachaise hips. Audrey is five-five. I'm five-seven. Jo is five-nine. Anything handed down from Audrey, we will it to work.

She refuses to spend major dollars on shoes. She buys her "skyscrapers" at Chandler's on Fifth Avenue. Audrey eschews the more outrageous styles—spectator riffs, jeweled embellishments or anything with see-through plastic—shoes that, by trying too hard, give themselves away. She opts for ornament-free, classically cut shoes that could have been purchased at I. Miller's across the street.

Handbags hail from Ohrbach's, their excellent European bag collection at West Thirty-fourth Street prices. Every night, she opens that day's handbag and extracts her French purse, comb, Shocking flacon, hankie, keys, lipstick, Stim-U-Dents, Pall Malls and matches. She lines them up on her vanity and wipes them down. She tosses her used hankie in the hamper and replaces it with a fresh one. Then she turns her handbag over and shakes the tobacco shreds into her mirrored wastebasket.

Prowling the Palazzo, Elsa finds a ladder that leads up to the attic. In an old trunk she discovers her mother's wedding dress and small lace-covered cushions she experiments with: "There were white pads that in my mother's youth women placed behind them, keeping them in place with string knotted in front, so that all the emphasis should be given to the curves of the behind and, in front, to their bosoms, which were held very high."

She spends hours alone, modeling long skirts and gowns, posing in front of a cheval mirror. Later, she uses this bustled, high-breasted silhouette again and again. It shows up in Muriel Spark's novel *The Girls of Slender Means:*

In wartime England, girls of slender means venture to

London to find jobs and romance. A private club is converted into dormitories. Despite rationing, spirits are high, love is topic number one, and everybody trades coupons. One of the girls has something the others covet: a "Schiaparelli taffeta evening dress which had been given to her by a fabulously rich aunt, after one wearing. . . . For lending it out Anne got various returns, such as free clothing coupons or a half-used piece of soap."

The dress is made

> with small side panniers stuck out with cleverly curved pads over the hips. It was coloured dark blue, green, orange and white in a floral pattern as from the Pacific Islands. [Nicholas] said, "I don't think I've ever seen such a gorgeous dress."
>
> "Schiaparelli," she said.
>
> He said, "Is that the one you swap amongst yourselves?"
>
> "Who told you that?"
>
> "You look beautiful," he replied.
>
> She picked up the rustling skirt and floated away up the staircase.

Toward the end of the novel, the Schiaparelli is stolen by Selina, who risks her life to retrieve it from a fire.

"Not very nice of her to pinch another girl's dress . . ." says the rector.

"It was a Schiaparelli dress."

On her twelfth birthday, Elsa is given a clothing allowance. She will be able to spend fifty lire a month and choose her own wardrobe. "This was not a great amount even in those days, but I managed to look very well on it. Planning things out on the principle of what we now call 'separates,' I managed to give the impression that I had a lot of clothes."

Twenty years later, walking her dachshund Nuts on his Shocking Pink leash through the streets of Paris, she looks like a wealthy, stylish woman. She is barely five feet tall, trim and well proportioned. She rarely leaves the house without a hat: the Monkey Hat, the Tiny Fedora, the Pancake, the Poker Chip, the Pin Cushion, the Igloo Hat, the Hide-and-Seek, Bicornes, Poke Bonnets and Hussar Toques, the Roman Helmet, the Matador, the Birdcage Hat with Singing Bird, Cones and Funnels, the visionary Television Hat. Feathered skullcaps and turbans. The Pencil Hat with a real pencil piercing the crown for jotting down bets at the track and the Inkwell Hat with a quill. There is a hat that looks like a lamb chop with a white patent-leather "panty" on the bone. Her most imitated hat is her simplest: a jersey tube sewn closed on one end and worn multiple ways, called the Mad Cap. One of her clients, Katharine Hepburn, popularizes it. In New York, a hat manufacturer names his hat company Madcaps and turns out thousands. Alfred Solomon becomes a multimillionaire and moves to Saratoga Springs. "Schiap did not make millions," she wrote, "she just got so tired of seeing it reproduced that she wished she had never thought of it. From all the shop windows, including the five-and-ten-cent stores, at the corner of every street, from every bus, in town and in the country, the naughty hat obsessed her, it winked at her from the bald head of a baby in a pram. That day she gave the order to her salesgirls to destroy every single one in stock, to refuse to sell it, and never mention it again." Mad

Caps live on. Would Schiap laugh or be outraged? Maternity wards send newborns home in her unsinkable design.

She thinks wigs are a brilliant idea. Antoine, the famous Parisian *coiffeur*, designs her three that are waterproof. Schiap skis in them instead of a hat: "I wore them in white, in silver, in red for the snow of St. Moritz, and would feel utterly unconscious of the stir they created." Others are more formal: "On a gala evening you send it to your coiffeur. No loss of time, no heat, no pins, no torture. It comes home beautiful and glamorous."

She is not afraid to wear her most outrageous designs, even her see-through dress: "Although I am very shy (and nobody will believe it), so shy that the simple necessity of saying 'Hallo' sometimes makes me turn icy cold, I have never been shy of appearing in public in the most fantastic and personal getup." She rattles expectations. She transgresses. Collaborating with Salvador Dalí, she takes his *Venus de Milo of the Drawers* and designs a suit with drawers for pockets. She puts fingernails on gloves and windmills on heads. She blurs the line between fashion and art. She lives the creative person's dream: Every time you're seeing it, you're seeing it a new way.

The major difference between Schiap's clothes and my mother's is, Schiap's are designed to draw attention to the clothes, not the face. Wearing her clothes is a performance, dressing as theater. Whether you are beautiful or not, when you enter a room wearing something designed by Elsa Schiaparelli, your clothes are the star. An unattractive woman and a beautiful woman become, for a moment, equals. What face could compete with the Tears Dress from her Circus Collection, fabric printed to look like human flesh flayed by a lion?

The image covering a living person's skin is her skin ripped off. Who even notices a face? A dress made of hanging flesh eighty years before Lady Gaga's meat dress.

"Two words have always been banned from my house—the word 'creation,' which strikes me as the height of pretentiousness, and the word 'impossible.' I kept in touch with the needs of the women who had confidence in me and tried to help them find their type. This I believe to be the principal secret of being well-dressed."

I love the way my mother dresses. I subject her to the same critical eye she uses on me. The difference is, I can't find anything wrong with how she looks. Not one thing. I'm proud of her appearance, as if her glory rubs off on me. But I suspect there can be more to what you wear, that fashion rules aren't fast and true. I don't want to dress like she does. I don't want to be a glamour-puss. Not that I want to be Debbie Reynolds either. What I want is, I want my clothes to have ideas. I want them to have meaning. I want my clothes, if I think about them during the day, to make me smile.

We are watching *What's My Line?* on television. The Mystery Guest signs in. A sweeping "S" is formed by a gloved hand loaded with bracelets. I'm riveted. I know that "S" from Audrey's bottles and boxes. Could it be? A "C" connects to the "S," then an "H," then "Schiaparelli" in white chalk fills the blackboard.

The three of us, Audrey, Jo Ann and I, sit next to each other on the couch. Elsa Schiaparelli is drenched in jewelry as if she's risen from Captain Cook's treasure chest. Elsa Schiaparelli! Our TV is black and white, but in my heart I know her shiny strapless dress and matching hat are Shocking Pink. Audrey plucks a Pall Mall shred off the tip of her tongue. She leans in as the Mystery Guest fields questions. Schiap tries to disguise her voice, but her laugh doesn't sound American. My sister and I are glad Dorothy Kilgallen has been replaced for the evening by Faye Emerson. We are sure Dorothy Kilgallen cheats. We are sure that when Miss Kilgallen raises her tiny chin she's peeking under the blindfold. After a few rounds of questions, Bennett Cerf closes in: "Would it be safe to say that you are based in Paris?"

"You gay-ting hot!" Schiap says.

Cerf nails it. The panelists fling off their masks. Schiap rises from the guest chair, sashays over to the panelists and, bowing slightly, shakes their hands.

"Humpf!" Audrey says. "Look at her back in that dress! Didn't anyone tell her? How could she not know? She's too old for a strapless! And that jewelry! She looks like Astor's pet horse. And frankly, girls, if you ask me, that hat doesn't work. Not at all!"

My sister and I will ourselves into Audrey's hand-me-downs (*left to right*: Cecil, Audrey, Jo Ann, Patty).

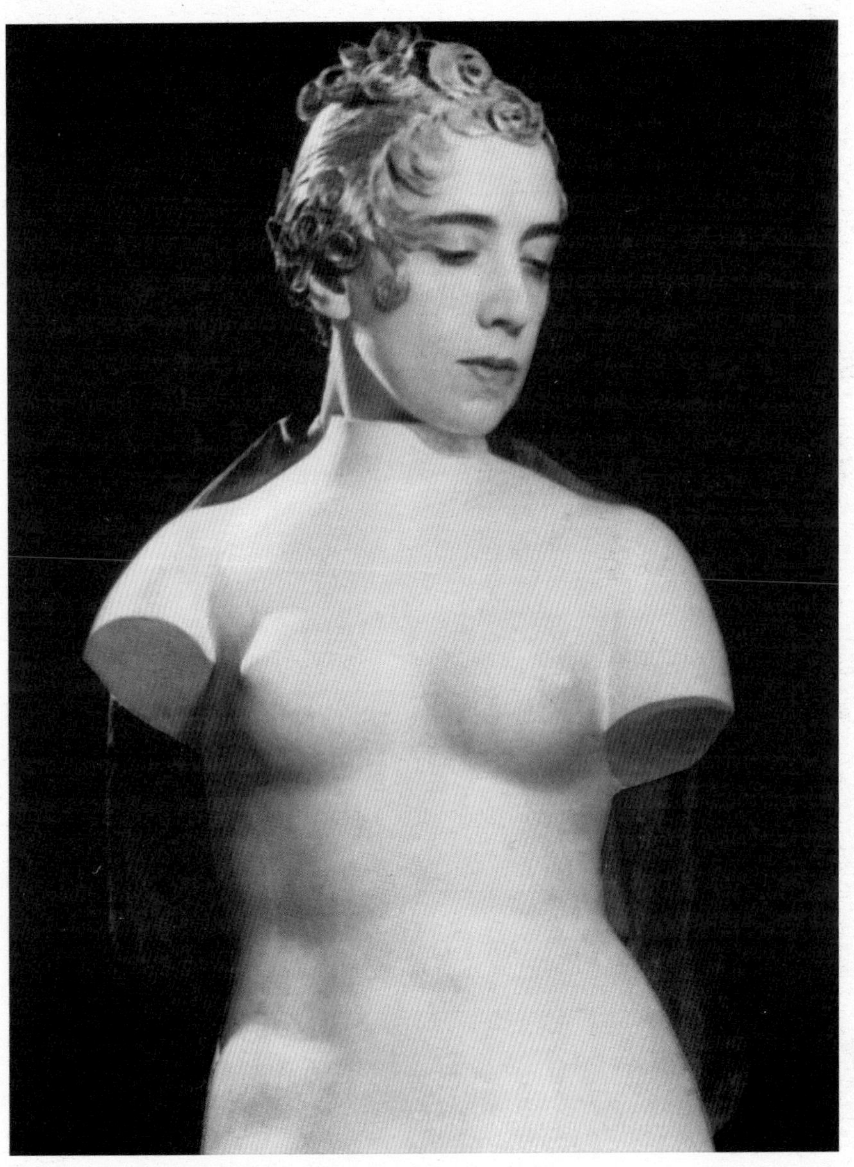

Man Ray's photo of Schiap in a wig designed by Antoine.

"The Desk Suit" had drawers for pockets and hardware for buttons. It was based on Dalí's *Venus de Milo of the Drawers.*

Katharine Hepburn, a client of the House of Schiaparelli, popularized Schiap's Mad Cap in America.

chapter seven

The Womanly Arts

It is the responsibility of a wife to
redecorate her home every ten years.

—*Audrey Volk*

I acquired nothing merely because of its value either in money or age. Therefore the house sings with a feeling of abandon, throws its arms around you, hugs you, and whoever comes to it to be a guest never wants to leave it.

—*Elsa Schiaparelli*

Whether she works or not, a woman has certain inviolate areas of expertise:

1. *A woman is responsible for running the home.*
   A smoothly run home is the province of the female. That is why she is called "the Lady of the House." A

My favorite Schiaparelli design: The Bug Necklace.
The bugs, made by Jean Schlumberger, crawled
around the neck on an invisible Rhodoid collar.

The Big Dipper is embroidered on this velvet dinner jacket from Schiap's 1938 Zodiac Collection.

"Le Roy Soleil." The features of the face are birds in flight, Schiap's symbol of freedom.

"Snuff" was the first perfume for men. The presentation came in a cigar box. The scent, in a glass pipe.

Schiap invented the backless dress and used it on her Butterfly Gown. To keep the butterflies from flying away, she trapped them in a Butterfly Net Coat. Furthering the Surrealist motif, she accessorized her ensemble with a matching parasol of free-flying butterflies.

Everything has the potential to delight. Even, say, a button.

A vase? Lovers kissing? Jean Cocteau drew this optical illusion for Schiap. Beading and embroidery by Lesage.

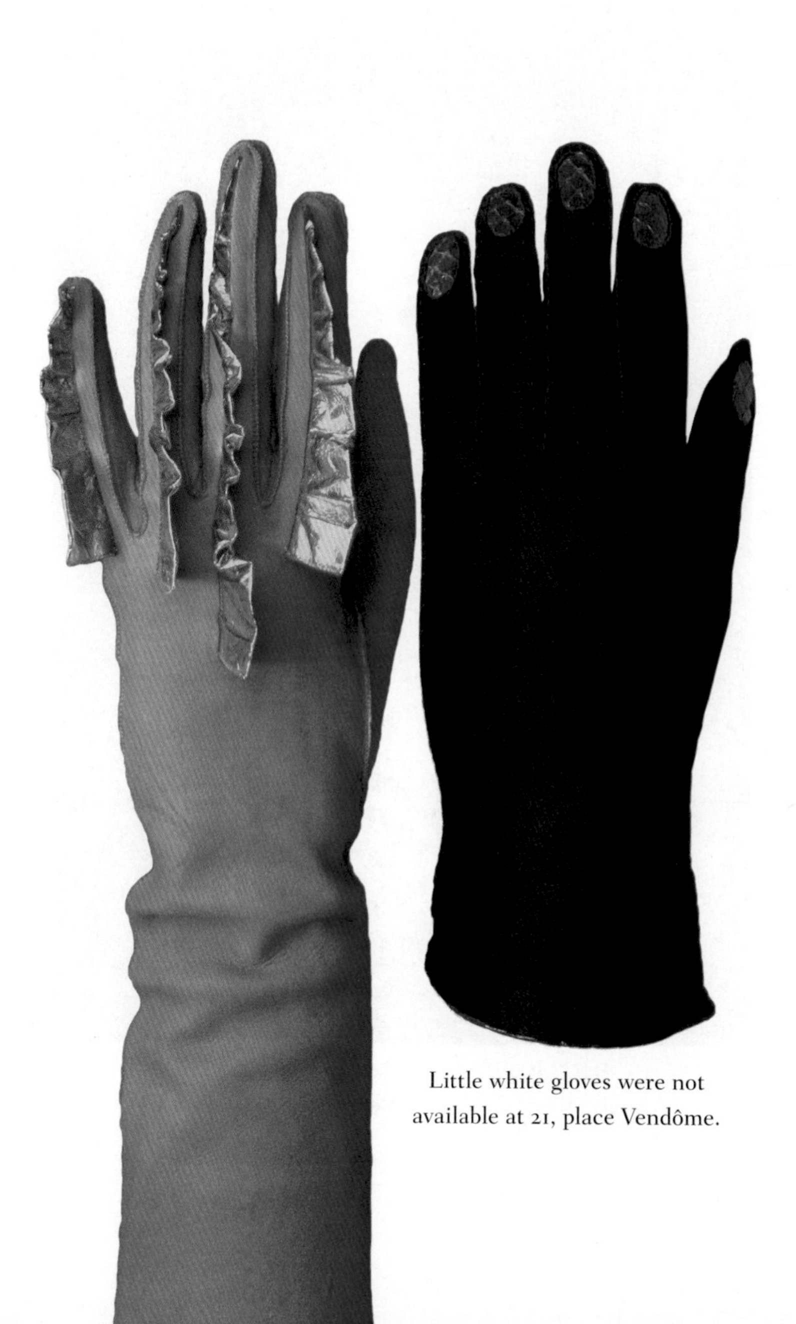

Little white gloves were not
available at 21, place Vendôme.

The Most Beautiful Woman in the World
in the World's Most Beautiful Necklace.

man has enough on his mind without being pestered to pick up milk or drop off dry-cleaning. It is understood that if it weren't for men, women wouldn't have a home to run. Men are unstintingly praised for their hard work:

"Have another slice, darling. You work so hard!"

"Here. Put your feet up. Isn't that better?"

"Let me get you that glass of water. You must be ex*hausted*!"

A woman makes all decisions regarding what her family eats and wears, standards of cleanliness, social engagements and child-rearing. She "lays out" her husband while he showers. That said, she doesn't "keep house." She runs her home by directing her housekeeper. In our case, that's Mattie Watts. Nana has Lily Brebner. Granny, Martha Wyjtola.

As soon as Schiap can afford it, she hires a married couple. They stay with her for twenty years. The wife does all the cooking except on Sunday nights. Sundays are reserved for friends Schiap calls "the chosen." On that night, Schiap herself cooks—pasta or an ox tongue with port—and invites as many as twenty. She gives them "the run of the house. They can use anything in it to put on shows—furs, underwear, kitchen utensils, jewels."

Greta Garbo, her friend and client, asks: "How is it that you allow these wonderful but crazy people the freedom of your possessions?" Schiap explains that they leave the house "in complete order, so that after they are gone my cupboards, my bathroom, and indeed every other corner of the house, are as tidy as if a fastidious maid had been at work."

I don't know what to make of this. Audrey doesn't like anyone to touch her things. If I borrow a blouse, it's mine.

She won't wear it again. She won't wear anything anyone else has worn.

2. *A woman must be adept at entertaining.*

When she entertains, which is frequently, Audrey sets the table with gold-monogrammed place plates, a gift from Granny Ethel. On top of those, she layers her favorite Herend Rothschild Bird china she got in Nassau "for a song." Mattie polishes the wedding flatware and George II cobalt saltcellars held aloft on the hairy hooves of silver goats. Candelabras light the table. An enormous gold jewelry-casket spills roses. A small wrapped present is laid to the left of everyone's water glass—perfume or a pretty pillbox for the ladies, knotted silk cufflinks or pocket squares for the men. Audrey is smitten with her stemware—water goblets, red-wine, white-wine and champagne coupes, twelve of each, forty-eight glasses purchased on the island of Murano, hand-blown, hand-carved, hand-gilt.

"These are Clara Petacci's glasses," she announces. "Clara Petacci had the same ones."

Why my mother is proud to have the same taste in stemware as Mussolini's mistress baffles. Everybody knows Mussolini was the enemy. Visiting her mother in Italy, Schiap turns down an invitation to meet him. Neighborhood kids sing a song to "Whistle While You Work":

Whistle while you work
Hitler is a jerk
Mussolini
Hit his peni
Now it doesn't squirt.

Party menus are a variation of what's served every day: Instead of steamed artichokes with brown butter, the hollow is filled with Hollandaise, a sure-hit appetizer. Rack of lamb *persillé* sits in for lamb chops or New York strip is replaced by my favorite, Tournedos Rossini. Plain asparagus morph into Asparagus Mimosa, baked potatoes into creamy, crusty Pommes Anna. Audrey's favorite dinner-party dessert is Baked Alaska accompanied by flaming Cherries Jubilee, surrealistic food, frozen and on fire at the same time. It takes two people to serve: one to hold, one to torch. On these evenings, Mattie wears a shiny black dress with white collar and cuffs and a white, heavily starched apron. She leans in smiling, serving to the left, gripping both ends of the silver well-and-tree, a wedding present from Aunt Gertie in flusher times. Guests slip Mattie a dollar when, as good-nights are made at the door, she materializes to help them with their coats.

Schiap entertains four ways: lavishly, casually, intimately and solo. For her formal Bal de Ballon, she has a hot-air balloon inflated in the center of her courtyard and hires a man who looks very much like the great balloonist Monsieur Auguste Piccard to sit in the basket all night long. She drapes the tables in Shocking Pink silk tartan and illuminates her trees with green and pink lights. For casual evenings, friends fill a real bistro with a zinc bar built into her basement. Politicians, artists, writers, whole dance companies come for cellar dinners after the show. Tables are set with gold-embroidered cloths and vermeil plates. Glasses are all different colors and shapes. "There is certainly something psychologically tantalizing in having good china, good linen and good food in a cellar." Schiap invents an oversize *tête-á-tête* for intimate dinners in her living room. A man and a woman can dine together, facing each other, with a tray between them, leaning back, legs extended in total comfort. But for her favorite soirée of all, when Schiap entertains Schiap alone, the librarian's daughter makes an actual written-down date with herself to spend the evening in her favorite room in the world, her library, a room with photographs of friends, "beloved paintings put anywhere, on the floor, on chairs, against ancient Chinese bronzes. Then there are books, books, books. . . ."

3. *A woman must play an instrument.*

Sheet music is kept in the piano bench of the same Hardman grand Audrey played as a little girl. We sing as she sight-reads the popular tunes of the day: "I Love Paris," "There's a Small Hotel," "Where, Oh Where (Is That Combination So Rare?)." She warms up with "I Can Dream, Can't I?," a song that starts with a thrilling glissando down the keyboard from the highest note to the lowest, hand over hand, until it ends in bold chords. When company comes, Audrey hoists me onto the piano lid and places a long chiffon scarf in my hand. I sing "Bewitched, Bothered and Bewildered" for her guests and flail the scarf. My act is followed by my sister's command performance of "Rondo alla Turque" with a "Minuet in G" encore. Jo takes piano lessons from Cosme McMoon, former bodybuilder and accompanist to the soprano Florence Foster Jenkins, who is cited in *The Incomplete Book of Failures: The Official Handbook of the Not-Terribly-Good Club of Great Britain* as "The Worst Singer." Mr. McMoon raps Jo's fingers with a Mongol pencil when she hits the wrong key. Lessons end on an up note.

Commandeering the piano bench, Cosme McMoon bangs out "Round Her Neck She Wore a Yellow Ribbon" for us to sing at the top of our lungs.

I'm not good enough for Mr. McMoon. I take lessons from Blanche Solomon, who lives crosstown, a two-bus commute. I'm not crazy about her neighborhood. One day, as I'm approaching her awning, someone with perfect timing dumps orange pulp on my head from a window. Mrs. Solomon doesn't like teaching me so she feeds me instead and we pass a strained hour with graham crackers and milk. She sits across from me at a red oilcloth–covered table in her kitchen. I ask why I can hear myself swallow if the action takes place inside my body. Mrs. Solomon gives me swallowing lessons. Time passes. We fill an hour. I fail to transcend "The Spinning Song."

Schiap loathes her piano lessons too. In *Shocking Life* she writes: "That was sheer agony. To sit on a stool, hitting the same note, was unbearable." She fakes hysterics after each lesson until her parents let her quit.

In 1939, Schiap presents her Music Collection. As usual, everything relates to the theme. A handbag opens, and a music box inside plinks "Rose Marie, I Love You." Another bag is shaped like an accordion. Belt buckles are hurdy-gurdies. Buttons, clips and hairpins are miniature violins, bagpipes and horns. The dresses themselves float with singing birds and buzzing bees. Music staves ripple with half-notes, grace notes and chords. This is the gown Schiap chooses for her daughter, Gogo, to wear to her first ball. It's organza, full-skirted and cut on the bias, a gown made for dancing. I show Mr. McMoon a picture of Gogo's dress and ask him to play the music on it. I'm certain Schiap left a secret message, that the notes will mean something. I'm hoping for "The Marseillaise" or "Dance, Ballerina, Dance."

Cosme McMoon plays the dress.

"What song is that?" I ask.

"This is fake music in A minor," he says. "The rhythm doesn't make any sense."

4. *Men lead. Women follow.*

There are four kinds of social dancers: natural, schooled, bad and the ones who learn to trust one partner exclusively. They perform well but only with that particular person. That is the kind of dancer Audrey is. In college, her dance card was filled. So at one time, she had diverse partners. But now she likes to dance only with Cecil. To watch her dance with another man at a party, to watch her compromise her ideals of perfection, is agony. She tries to engage the partner in a heated discussion so the emphasis is less on dancing. If the conversation gets intense enough, they can stop dancing yet remain on the floor, loosely clasping each other, talking as if what they have to say is much more important than the act of dancing and requires complete concentration. Most of the time, Audrey resigns herself to the rigors of following. She tosses her head with confidence, as if it's her partner's fault they fail to mesh. Cecil doesn't ask other women to dance unless Audrey chooses to sit one out. Then I get to watch him pull out all the stops. He glides across the floor. He swirls, dips and breaks away. Another woman "reads" his signals. Dancers give them room. He laughs. The woman laughs too. I check my mother's reaction. Her face idles in neutral.

Audrey sends me to Helen Rigby's for tap, Madame Svoboda's for ballet and, for social dancing, the Viola Wolff School of the Dance. Boys and girls wear party clothes and white gloves. I'm the tallest girl in the class and there aren't enough boys so I have to lead. Young Roman girls of Elsa's class study social dancing too. At the fashionable Scuola di Pichetti, they learn Le Quadrille des Lanciers, a figured dance from the 1820s, when lances were beginning to be used by the cavalry. Four pairs of dancers face each other. There are five "figures," or movements: the Promenade, Moulinets, Chevaux de Bois, the Passe and the Corbelle. Partners are honored, corners are honored, there are deep dips, salutes, bows and curtsies. Advancements speed up as the figures progress. Quadrilles are highly choreographed and formal. They sound like more fun than the waltz. They sound like square dances, which I love. Schiap learns only the quadrille. The first time a man asks her to tango at a ball, she's at a loss. It turns out she's a natural. In the 1930s in Paris, women dance with women. At Le Bal de Forêt, Coco Chanel comes as Chanel, but Schiap rises to the occasion as a Surrealist oak tree. Chanel spots her amid a throng of admirers. She doesn't like Schiap. Her favorite clients, Nancy Cunard and Daisy Fellowes, have jilted her for the House of Schiaparelli.

Chanel taps Schiap on the shoulder. *"Voulez-vous danser?"*

The oak tree and Chanel begin an energetic fox-trot.

Leading, Chanel backs Schiap into a bank of lit candles. Her bark ignites. Guests grab soda siphons and extinguish Schiaparelli.

5. *A woman must sew.*

When Audrey is little, Polly designs and makes her clothes by hand. Dresses with georgette collars. Graduation gowns.

A green velvet coat with Persian-lamb trim. Polly Morgen is what is called "good with a needle." Audrey can sew too. It is a wife's responsibility to maintain her husband's socks. When one of Cecil's develops a hole in the heel, Audrey repairs it. Her sewing box is a square duplex woven like a basket. Tidy spools of jewel-colored thread line up in the top story. From the basement she locates her darning egg. It looks like a rattle. She slips the round end down the neck of the sock until it stretches the hole in the heel. Her stitches are neat. She picks up one thread of still-woven sock (the third one in from the hole) and loops her needle under it, connecting it to a partner of still-intact sock on the other side of the hole. She draws sock and thread together, pulling them lightly, just so, to mimic the tension of extant sock, over and over, north to south, east to west, until the hole disappears beneath a scab of thread. Audrey excels at socks, name tapes and buttons. Anything more arduous—a hem, a seam—goes to the dressmaker.

Years later I teach a class in contemporary culture to aspiring actors at the Tisch School at NYU. We discuss superannuation. I bring in Audrey's darning egg.

"What do you think this is?" I ask, holding it up. They pass it around.

"A maquette for a Brancusi?" one says.

"You use it to make guacamole!"

"A massager?"

"Does anyone know what 'darning' means?" No one does. Their socks are disposable. They laugh when I tell them people used to repair socks.

While Audrey darns, I unscrew her button jar. It's a Hellmann's mayonnaise jar, thirty-two-ounce size, heavy with the buttons of her life. I shake them out on her quilt. Buttons from clothes she wore and buttons that come as spares in tiny envelopes once attached to new clothes. There are white glass flower buttons the size of Oreos, mauve silk balls from her engagement dress, buttons that look like heraldic shields, lace-covered buttons, various sizes of tortoiseshell buttons with rolled rims, mother-of-pearl buttons, shirt buttons, rhinestone buttons, clear plastic buttons, buttons like knotted gold rope, a pink silk faille button from her Claire McCardell dress with the buttoned cummerbund, horn buttons, toggles, rainbow abalone, navy reefer buttons with anchors on them. Most buttons I know from her suits and dresses. Some are from before my time. Carved amber ones belonged to my great-grandmother. There are buttons that look like bows and domed gold ones with raised eagles. There are faceted black buttons, set in prongs, kept together on a string. My favorite looks like a tiny bunch of grapes. It has leaves.

"What's this one from, Ma?"

She looks up from her work. "The grapes? That was from my going-away suit, darling. Part of my trousseau."

Not until I'm older do I learn the word for the pleasant longing I feel touching these buttons. It is "nostalgia."

Polly teaches me how to sew. She asks me to thread her needle for company.

"Did you ever in your life see such a child? She got it on the first try!"

My sister, who has also learned to sew from Nana, teaches me the chain stitch.

I make Audrey macaroni necklaces, Popsicle-stick frames and ashtrays out of clay. But when I turn ten, I'm allowed to cross the street myself. I can walk to Woolworth's. I walk from Eighty-third and Riverside Drive to Broadway and Seventy-ninth to buy my mother a hankie for Mother's Day. I'm going to monogram it with red thread. "A" for "Audrey." I will use the chain stitch. My allowance is fifty cents a week. Hankies at Woolworth's are ten. I can buy my mother a present and still have enough for a thirty-five-cent hot-fudge sundae at Schrafft's with a five-cent tip.

I buy a white hankie. Sewing the "A," I pull the thread too tight. The fabric bunches. I flush the hankie down the toilet.

The next day after school, I walk back to Woolworth's.

The second hankie, when I finish it, you can see the ballpoint ink I drew the "A" in. I flush that one too.

The third hankie I use a pencil. The lead rubs off on the thread, turning it black. The toilet overflows.

I want the hankie to be perfect. My mother is perfect.

"*Another* hankie?" the saleslady at Woolworth's says.

Back home I thread the needle. I begin to chain-stitch. This one looks good. Then I try to iron it. The front is sewn to the back. I throw it out the window.

I am down to my last dime. On the fifth hankie the stitches on the crossbar of the "A" don't match the vertical ones even though I've used the chain stitch on both. That hankie sails out the window too.

I borrow ten cents from my sister. I have to give her an IOU for fifteen cents. Hankie number six, when I bite the thread off, it pulls a hole.

Now my sister wants a twenty-cent IOU for one last dime. I draw the "A" on a piece of paper first, then Scotch-tape the paper to the window. Next I Scotch-tape the hankie over the paper. Light comes through. I can see the penciled "A" through the cloth. I use the needle to wiggle tiny holes where the stitches should go. I prick my finger. Blood gets on the hankie. I fill the sink with hot water and let the hankie soak. Yellow gum from the Scotch tape melts into the hankie.

The doorbell rings. Tom the doorman wants to know if someone from our apartment is throwing hankies out the window.

On Mother's Day, I serve Audrey breakfast in bed.

Invited to her first Parisian ball, Schiap buys four yards of dark blue crêpe de chine at Galeries Lafayette and two yards of orange silk. She's twenty-three. She doesn't know how to sew. She drapes the blue over, under, around and through, turning herself into a Zouave. She keeps everything together with hidden pins and a bright-orange sash. What's left of the orange fabric is wound into a turban. This is Elsa Schiaparelli's first creation. It causes a sensation. And then she is asked to dance. Something is wrong. She feels herself unraveling. Her escort tangos her out the door. Schiap never does learn to sew. The woman profiled three times in *The New Yorker,* who will one day be the subject of retrospectives at the Philadelphia Museum of Art and the Met, the woman who calls herself "a maker of dresses," can't make a dress? This violates a basic Audrey tenet: If you want to be good at something, you must learn it from the bottom up. You play

"From a Rose" before you play "Für Elise." You sketch before you paint. You master the Five Positions before you execute an arabesque. In a house of couture, according to Audrey, Schiap would start as an *arpette,* whose job is to pick pins off the floor. But Schiap sketches her designs or points to pictures in art books to describe what she wants and her staff does the rest. She critiques each phase. Adjustments are made. The most famous couturier in the world doesn't know the basics. What's more, she believes *not* knowing them makes her better at what she does. "Schiap decidedly did not know anything about dressmaking," Schiap writes. "Her ignorance in this matter was supreme. Therefore her courage was without limit and blind."

Like Audrey, Schiap takes a great interest in buttons. She uses them to comment on the dress. She's driven to pump the most out of an idea, to take it beyond expectation. At the House of Schiaparelli, "King Button" reigns: "The most incredible things were used, animals and feathers, caricatures and paperweights, chains, locks, paper clips, and lollipops." Buttons like hand mirrors let you freshen your lipstick by looking down. Owls! Swans! Bugs! Nuts! Suns! Moons! Stars! Cinnamon sticks and licorice! Buttons are not ordered from suppliers. Schiap would rather give artists work—Alberto Giacometti, René Clément, Jean Schlumberger, Leonor Fini, Meret Oppenheim. A button can be art. Commercial buttons? A missed opportunity. Why settle for functional when a button could be life-enhancing. No detail is trivial. A Schiaparelli button has to amuse and surprise. Everything—all of it, her home, her designs, her perfume presentations, her boutiques—is infused with one reigning principle: Everything has the potential to delight. Even, say, a button.

6. *A woman is responsible for the look of her home.*

Lee Epstein is the family decorator. Audrey and Polly are besotted by her taste. Mrs. Epstein is the height of an eight-year-old. She wears only black and keeps her gray bangs immobilized by a pillbox hat. People say, "She's a dynamo!," something I notice is said only about short women. Lee Epstein is known for her "shot of color" look. She creates a monotone room, then visually startles you. Polly's living room is all yellow—yellow couch, yellow wall-to-wall, yellow chairs, yellow walls—then suddenly, just when your eyes are relaxing into yellowness, they light on a tiny ballroom chair covered in peacock-blue shantung. It's a jolt in the happiest sense of the word. In Audrey's all-cocoa living room—cocoa couch, cocoa walls, cocoa carpet—two club chairs are chartreuse. Her bedroom is emerald green except for a puffy rose satin quilt with trapunto so deep you could lose a finger tracing it. Everybody raves. Later my mother will shift to a decorator who is known for upholstered walls and trompe-l'oeil finishes. His specialty is making new furniture look old. He strips a bureau to bare wood, has it repainted, has the new paint partially rubbed off, then hits it with a hammer and drills it full of wormholes.

Audrey redecorates, stem to stern, once per decade. She keeps her wedding furniture—the Syrie Maugham sofa, her fauteuil and Louis XIV chairs—but has them reupholstered and refinished. Carpets are pulled up and replaced by rugs. Rugs are rolled up and replaced by wall-to-wall. Drapes are donated to Aunt Gertie. There is a new color scheme, all blue in the sixties, then lots of polished floral chintz with fluffy tassels in the seventies. The eighties brought muted pastels. In a move that surprises, before she relocates to her last home, Audrey jettisons every memory-soaked piece. In Florida she buys the developer's spec house. Whenever she buys a house, she buys a spec house: "I like to know what I'm getting," she says. "I like *fresh*." A decorator from the Boca Raton Bloomingdale's is engaged, and in one day they furnish the biggest house of Audrey's life, from teaspoons to sheets to zebra-skin rugs, couches, patio furniture and a Ming dynasty horse. French polished mahogany and ormolu are replaced by Lucite, chrome and leather. Two weeks later, a semi pulls into the driveway. Everything is delivered the same day. Every room in the new house feels like a model room in a department store. It is a home without anything personal, pared down, no history, and it thrills my parents. It renews them. They don't miss a thing.

Schiap hires Jean-Michel Frank to decorate her first apartment. He commissions Dalí to make a footstool out of the hip bones of a horse. Alberto Giacometti casts plaster sconces and lamps. Diego Giacometti forges tables. In the living room, an enormous orange leather couch faces "two low armchairs in green. The walls are white and the curtains and chair covers are made of a white rubber substance that was stiff and gleaming." When she moves to her mansion on the rue de Berri, Schiap does a one-eighty. Audrey went from traditional to modern. Schiap abandons modern for what she grew up with: pattern on pattern, paintings over paintings, artifacts, bibelots, taxidermy, divans and bergères. Jean-Michel Frank insists she get rid of her François Boucher chinoiserie tapestry. Schiap refuses. They lock horns. Finally Frank gives in. Then he makes the tapestry disappear by painting the other walls in the room with trompe-l'oeil copies of it so the real one doesn't stand out. Boucher paints a painting. Gobelins weaves a tapestry of the Boucher painting. Frank has murals painted from the Gobelins tapestry of the Boucher painting. The rooms on the rue de Berri are layered. They have no negative space. The eye is kept in motion. These rooms are added to but they are not redone. Everything has meaning.

Clara Petacci's stemware.

The world-famous French balloonist Monsieur Auguste Piccard.

My sister's piano teacher, Cosme McMoon, former bodybuilder and accompanist to Florence Foster Jenkins. Part of his job was retrieving roses Mrs. Jenkins had strewn during matinees so she could re-strew them that evening.

Polly made Audrey a green velvet coat with
Persian-lamb trim and a matching hat.

Not a maquette for a Brancusi.
Not for making guacamole.
Not a massager.

For easy reference, Mom tied her dance cards around her wrist.

chapter eight

Friendship

> If a friend hurts you on purpose, it's because she's jealous. Feel sorry for her. If she hurts you unintentionally, feel sorry for her. She is crass.
>
> —*Audrey Volk*

> Believing tremendously in friendship, she expects too much of her friends: sheer disappointment in their capacity to respond has often made her enemies. Flattery and small talk bore her . . . and though she was helped mostly by other women she got along better with men.
>
> —*Elsa Schiaparelli*

Friends are essential but Audrey is firm:

"Never have a best friend, darling. Never put all your eggs in one basket."

She heeds her advice but hedges her bet. She doesn't have one best friend, she has four. We call them "Aunt." To call an adult by a first name is impertinent and "Mrs." too formal for people we kiss.

Aunt Dorothy, Aunt Horty, Aunt Ruth and Aunt Honey form the best-friend galaxy. Aunt Ruth is Audrey's best friend from high school. During Christmas break, Ruth marries her uncle. She returns to class in a mink coat she takes off only for gym. Ruth and Audrey remain best friends through Ruth's five husbands. By husband three, she's gotten a new nose, contact lenses, has lost weight and gone blonde and suddenly Aunt Ruth is gorgeous in a peppy Jane Powell way. By husband five, she owns a stable. Aunt Ruth has primate dental spacing—little spaces between her teeth like chimps. Primate spacing keeps Aunt Ruth looking young even when she has to use oxygen at the track.

Aunt Dorothy is genteel, a Cornell graduate who speaks flawless French. She invites us to her island in the Adirondacks every summer. The couples vacation together and attend the New York Valedictory Ball every year, triple-dating with Dorothy's in-laws. We go to Madame Svoboda's Ecole de Ballet and Camp Red Wing with Susie and Nancy, Dorothy's daughters, our oldest friends, friends since Dorothy and Audrey were pregnant together, friends since utero.

Aunt Honey tells me something I can't get over: "I was five when I met Albert and knew I would marry him." She's in show business, a Broadway star. Aunt Honey sings "Bali H'ai" in *South Pacific* and costars as Mother Burnside and Madame Branislowski opposite Angela Lansbury in *Mame*. At Audrey's parties, Uncle Albert plays the piano and they lean into each other on the bench, harmonizing to "Baby, It's Cold Outside." The house fills with music. A Broadway star at our piano. Of the four "aunts," I laugh most with Aunt Honey.

Audrey discovers Aunt Horty in Sidney Hook's philosophy class at NYU: "I looked around the room for someone who looked like me, and there she was, looking back."

Both are beautiful. Both are five feet five, slender and love to "dress." They whoosh into parties in starched crinolines and attend luncheons in sheaths and hats. They take cruises together with their husbands, who are best friends too. They are reverse images of each other: Aunt Horty has black hair and white skin. Audrey is blonde and tan. They speak on the phone every day before getting out of bed. Mattie carries in a tray—fresh orange juice, toast and coffee. Then Audrey and Aunt Horty smoke, talk and have breakfast together. At the end of the day, before dinner, they catch up again. This time the tray ferries tea. We envy Aunt Horty. Audrey loves her so much. Audrey uses her beguiling voice when she talks to Horty. Aunt Horty is the only friend Audrey quotes:

"Aunt Horty says you should never cut your cuticles. Push them down with an orange stick."

"Aunt Horty says if you turn off the TV you have to wait a minute before turning it back on."

"Aunt Horty says the pizza at Ray's is better than the pizza at Joe's."

When air conditioning becomes available in cars, "Aunt Horty says you should turn it on and leave the door open and the car will get cooler much faster."

"Cooler faster than if the door is closed, Ma?"

"That's what Aunt Horty says."

Over the course of a sixty-four-year friendship, they take cha-cha lessons together, play bridge together, move from New York to Kings Point, Long Island, together then thirty-three years later, sell those homes and retire to Boca

Raton together. One winter, they rent a motel room in East Hampton for a week and give up smoking together. They have three major falling-outs, extended periods when something goes haywire and they're not "on speaking terms." During these nadirs, Audrey is valiant but subdued. No laughter ripples from her bedroom. No Pall Malls are lit when the telephone rings. "Your Aunt Horty says . . . " and all Aunt Horty references are banished from conversation. We are not told Audrey and Horty are on the outs. We don't have to be. Loss permeates the air. Our mother is inconsolable and there's nothing we can do about it. The worst silent treatment lasted a year. But usually, after a few months of mourning, one of them picks up the phone and, without discussing the injury, they start talking as if nothing has happened. Once again my mother's step is light. She calls us "darling" again and we know it's okay to say, "What's new with Aunt Horty?" As they age though, a peculiar thing happens: Audrey spurns Horty. When Horty comes to visit in the hospital, Audrey screams through the canvas curtain: "Did I invite you, Hortense? Did anybody ask you to come? Go home!" Then she turns on Horty's husband. She's tired of him talking about his father "as if he were Abraham Lincoln." She's angry he's not more grateful to Cecil for including him in all-guy sorties. She ridicules him for buying dental instruments to scale his own teeth and mocks them both when they split the pork-chop entrée at Houston's. She complains that when she plays devil's advocate Horty doesn't bite. Audrey can't get a rise. This goads my mother, makes her a little nuts. She delights in verbal sparring. She has a gift for it. She hurls herself against the barbed wire of dissonance and volunteers for either side. I begin thinking of her as "The Arbiter of Everything" after she excommunicates Cecil's buddy Irv. Irv helps himself to a banana from Audrey's fruit bowl, breaks off half, bandages the remains with flappy peel, then drops it back in the bowl. There is a right way and a wrong way to eat a banana when you're a guest in someone's house. Audrey refuses to go out with Irv and his wife, Shelly, again.

Post-banana, she turns on all her friends except Fran and Muriel. No one could turn on Muriel, beautiful, generous, a natural at keeping it light. If Audrey were to say, "Hitler had a good side," Muriel would respond, "You don't say, darling. Is that so?" Audrey doesn't turn on Fran either. Fran has a world-class brain. Audrey respects that. Of all Audrey's friends, these last two need her the least. Audrey can smell need a mile away.

"Don't mix your friends," she warns.

Audrey is orthodox about her best friends not being friends with each other. What if they make dates that exclude her? What if they leave her out? Meeting without Audrey, they could talk behind her back. When she introduces friends to each other, if they subsequently meet without inviting her, Audrey drops them both. She claps her hands, wiping one off against the other, and says: "Well, I've crossed *her* off my list!"

Procedure for dropping a friend:

"Don't return calls. If she corners you at a party or on the street, say, 'Darling, forgive me. I've been meaning to call you. I'll call you tonight.' Then don't. Never discuss why the friendship has failed. Character is immutable—what's the point? After a while," Audrey says, "she'll get the message."

Once Audrey cuts a friend, that friend is dead to her. If one of my friends hurts me, that friend's dead to her too.

Decades after I've forgotten a slight, Audrey will say, "What? You're having lunch with Judy Fram? She didn't invite you to her Sweet Sixteen!" Or "Alice Immerman? How could you? That girl never returned your comics!"

Audrey does not confide anything to a friend she minds being repeated. But lest friends think your life is perfect, "once in a while you have to throw them a bone." She digs into her bone box and flings:

"Oh, that Cecil. He spent all day Saturday at Ghost Motorcycles!"

"Patty came home an hour after curfew! I paced a hole in the rug!"

"I've forbidden Jo Ann to see Eddie Oliphant again!"

She offers these tidbits as gifts, tiny personal problems to suggest that, contrary to what you might think, her life isn't flawless.

It surprises me when she says: "There is no such thing as a friendship between a man and a woman. It isn't possible." She's adamant: "It's never neutral for a man, darling, *never.* It *can't* be. A platonic friendship between a man and a woman? *Please.*"

I don't believe her. There are boys I love. But there are many more I like, boys I ride my bike and play handball with, boys I *don't* think about before falling asleep.

Schiap has plenty of men friends too—Marcel Duchamp, Alfred Stieglitz, the Giacomettis, Edward Steichen, Christian "Bébé" Bérard, Jean-Michel Frank, Marcel Vertès, Raoul Dufy, Cecil Beaton. Paul Poiret dresses her for free when she has no money. Salvador Dalí is a close friend *and* collaborator. New to Paris, it's Man Ray who escorts her to the hottest club in town. At Le Boeuf sur le Toit, he introduces Schiap to other men who become friends: Picasso, Maurice Chevalier, André Gide, Jean Cocteau, the Prince of Wales, Erik Satie.

Man Ray, Bébé, Duchamp, Dalí—her closest friends are men. Women find her to be "an enigma." From ten o'clock in the morning till closing, her workdays at 21, place Vendôme pass in a whirl of women. She develops Elsa Schiaparelli's Twelve Commandments for them:

I. Since most women do not know themselves they should try to do so.
II. A woman who buys an expensive dress and changes it, often with disastrous result, is extravagant and foolish.
III. Most women (and men) are color-blind. They should ask for suggestions.
IV. Remember—twenty percent of women have inferiority complexes. Seventy percent have illusions.
V. Ninety percent are afraid of being conspicuous, and of what people will say. So they buy a gray suit. They should dare to be different.
VI. Women should listen and ask for competent criticism and advice.
VII. They should choose their clothes alone or in the company of a man.
VIII. They should never shop with another woman, who sometimes consciously, and often unconsciously, is apt to be jealous.
IX. She should buy little and only of the best or the cheapest.
X. Never fit a dress to the body, but train the body to fit the dress.

XI. A woman should buy mostly in one place where she is known and respected, and not rush around trying every new fad.
XII. And she should pay her bills.

Schiap is as generous to young women as Poiret was to her. "June in Paris was Ball Month," Rosamond Bernier, art lecturer, *Vogue* editor and creator of *L'Oeil* magazine tells me over dinner. "There was a ball every night. Schiap lent me anything I wanted and I would return each gown, wrapped in tissue, at dawn the next morning, before the streets were swept."

Ms. Bernier's Metropolitan Museum of Art lectures are riveting, sold-out phenomena delivered in gowns by Schiaparelli, Balenciaga and Zandra Rhodes. When I can't get tickets for the one about Picasso and Matisse, I make an appointment with the Costume Institute and donate a pair of my great-great-aunt Bertha's Schiaparelli gloves. They are opera-length black suede, open-worked with diamante-studded silk mesh. Gants Jouvin, Schiap's favorite glovemaker, made them and they look like something Lady Macbeth would wear. Great-Great-Aunt Bertha was four feet ten, officially a midget. There's no way I can wedge my hands into her gloves. It seems like a good idea, a pair of unwearable Schiaparelli gloves for a pair of tickets to Rosamond Bernier.

"I'm so sorry," the Costume Institute assistant tells me, folding conservation paper around them. "We can't possibly get you tickets for Ms. Bernier. Thank you so much for the gloves."

I write to Ms. Bernier cold and tell her the story. She sends me two tickets.

During her final lecture at the Met, Rosamond Bernier describes sharing a compartment with Schiap on a train en route to Saint-Moritz: "It was an arduous trip. From a suitcase Schiap retrieved a smaller suitcase. It was her traveling martini bar, complete with olives, gin and vermouth. It had a silver shaker, martini glasses and a stirrer as well. The rest of the trip was more enjoyable."

At a later date, I ask Ms. Bernier if she and Schiap were good friends. She takes her time answering. "Schiap was very good company. She was funny. But she was not one to let women get close to her. She did not reveal herself in any way."

Audrey and "Aunt" Horty on a cruise with their husbands.

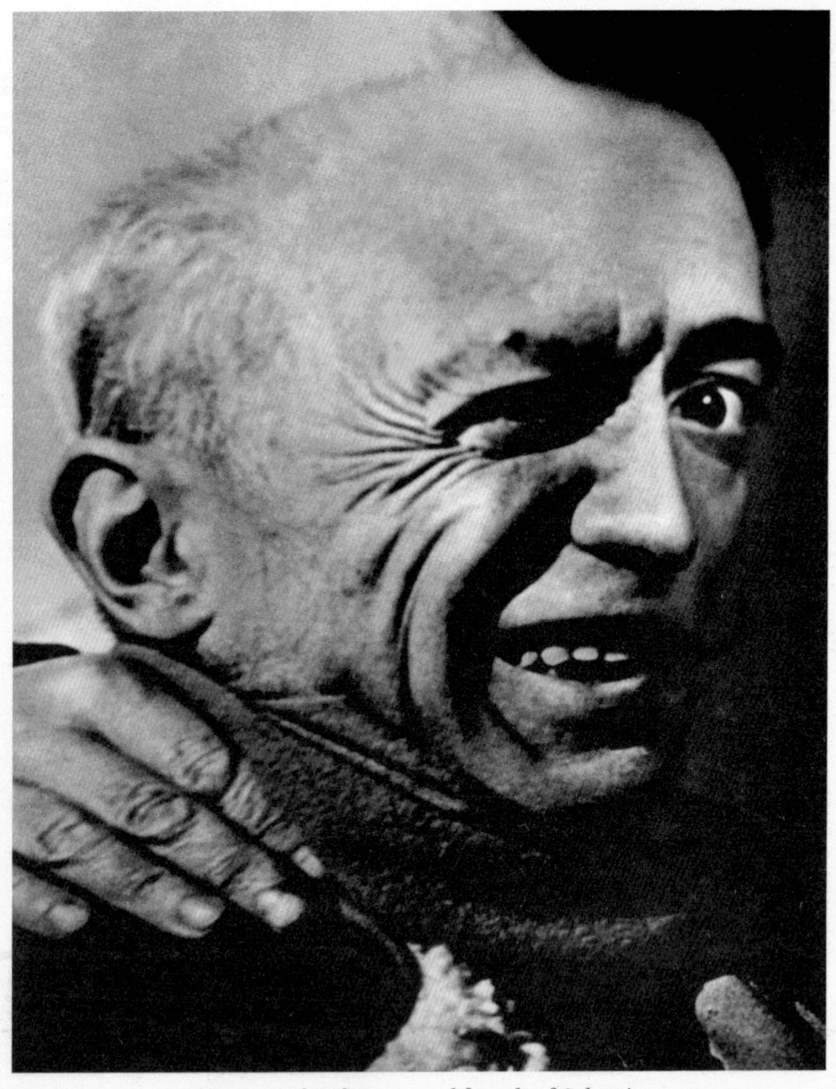

Picasso and Dalí were good friends of Schiap's.
Their work hung at 22, rue de Berri.

ROSAMOND BERNIER

7 March 1987

Miss Patricia Volk
1136 Fifth Avenue
New York, N.Y. 10128

Dear Miss Volk:

How can I resist such a plea!

I am sending you two of my private stock of tickets for the lecture series, and I will forward your check to the Metropolitan Museum.

Kindly be sure to phone the Metropolitan Museum office of Concerts and Lectures if for any reason you shall not be attending any of the lectures; they like to offer these "no-shows" at the door.

I hope you enjoy Picasso-Matisse.

Sincerely,

Rosamond Bernier /gjg

Rosamond Bernier

/gjg

166 EAST 61 STREET NEW YORK, NEW YORK 10021 (212) 759 2142

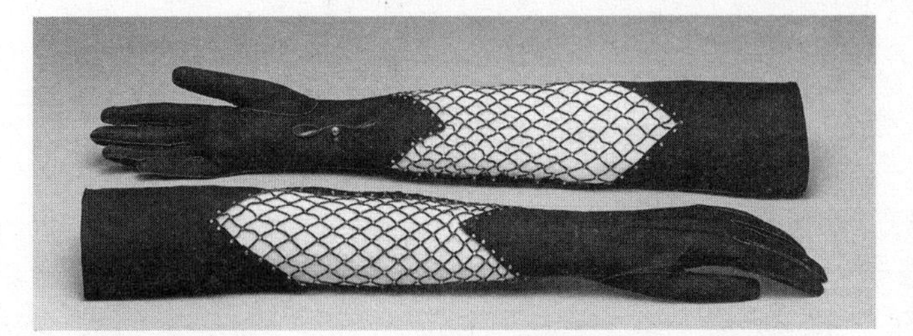

Gloves

Elsa Schiaparelli (Italian, 1890–1973)

Date: 1940s

Culture: French

Medium: leather, rhinestones, silk

Dimensions: Length: 23½ in. (59.7 cm)

Credit Line: Gift of Patricia Volk, 1986

Accession Number: 1986.189a, b

Schiaparelli gloves donated to the Metropolitan Museum in hope of getting tickets to hear Rosamond Bernier. It didn't work. The story had a happy ending anyway.

chapter nine

Lingerie

Don't neglect your sachets. At least twice a year, refresh them with perfume.

—*Audrey Volk*

The most modern falsies are called "Very Secret" and they are blown up with a straw, as if you are sipping crème de menthe.

—*Elsa Schiaparelli*

First you pull up triple-thick training pants. "Accidents" behind you, it's white cotton undies, elastic at the waist. Because you are learning to take care of your things yourself and because you are learning to read, each pair is embroidered with a day of the week: *Monday, Tuesday, Wednesday, Thursday, Friday, Saturday, Sunday*. Days-of-the-week undies are followed by white cotton Lollipops purchased at Rappaport's on Broadway. Lollipops (currently

$21.95 for a three-pack at vermontcountrystore.com) come up to the waist, like Marilyn Monroe's in *The Seven Year Itch*. There is a dramatic shift from cotton to nylon when you "fall off the roof" or "your aunt Tillie comes to visit" or you're "unwell." You stop calling them "undies." Overnight they become "panties." Nylon is easier to rinse than cotton. You are postpubescent and for the first time given money to purchase your own. You buy your first pair in a color other than white. Probably you get pink. It will be years before you catch on to black. You begin to understand the meaning of "Menopause ends thirty-five straight years of staring into your underpants."

Women did not start wearing true underpants until the early nineteenth century. Before then, knee-length leggings tied at the waist like chaps. Private parts were exposed. Half a century later, my grandmothers swore by woolies in winter, pink knit Bermuda shorts that thwarted life-threatening drafts. Under suits and sleek dresses, suppressive all-in-ones reigned. They were particular about their underwear, Polly and Ethel. They had corsetieres and believed that even if something is not seen by anyone besides the wearer, it behooves the wearer to have it pristine. Scrupulous underwear sets the tone from the bottom up. Polly drives this home with a true story. Life lessons are deployed as true-life stories. It is important to Nana that the victim of the story is someone she knows personally or a famous person. This removes the story from the realm of "hearsay."

Our family instructs via cautionary tale. The first time Audrey feeds me cherries she says, "Never stick a cherry pit up your nose. Your great-grandmother did, and a year later she sneezed and a vine came out of her nostril."

I never stick a cherry pit up my nose.

"Never swallow chewing gum. I went to school with a girl whose insides stuck together and she had to have surgery."

"Never push down garbage with your hand. Mrs. Blaine's aunt severed the artery in her wrist on a tin can and nearly bled to death."

"Always wear socks with your sneakers. Calvin Coolidge's son died from a blister."

There was The Man Who Swam Out Beyond the Buoy and Got Diced by a Propeller, and The Little Girl Who Gave a Squirrel a Peanut and Died from Rabies.

"Always wear clean underwear, because you never know when you'll get hit by a truck" is the horror story about Mrs. Wald in Apartment 12F. When she got divorced, her settlement was barely adequate. She went from wearing lingerie hand-made by nuns in France to buying her panties at Woolworth's for less a pair than she'd paid a laundress to hand-wash her old ones. Pretty soon, she couldn't afford those. But, like some people, Mrs. Wald thought if she could present to the world an outer look of elegance it didn't matter about her underthings.

Then one day while crossing the street, Mrs. Wald was hit by a truck. Unconscious, she was taken by ambulance to the nearest hospital. The director of the emergency room took one look at Mrs. Wald's outer finery and realized he was in the presence of someone important. Reluctantly, he cut through her clothes to facilitate the examination. When he saw the shabby state of her underwear, he assigned her to a first-year resident. She still limps.

Today underpants come in hipsters, thongs, bikinis, string bikinis, tangas, high-rise, low-rise, extra-low-rise, butt-enhancing, butt-suppressing, butt-*dividing,* boy shorts, girdle-like, disposable, edible, full-figure and, thanks to Frederick's of Hollywood, once again crotchless. The most disgruntled underwear people on the Internet can be found at mormoncurtain.com. Mormons are expected to wear "holy garments" during sex and giving birth. A woman can wear a bra, but she has to wear the garments underneath it. The holy garments are a "spiritual shield against the powers of Satan" and provide maximum coverage. Mormoncurtain .com is the site for people who no longer believe in "the magic power of the temple drawers." These people are angry. They refer to Brigham Young as Breedem Young.

"Mom told me, '*Never* go in my dresser. *Never* open my closet,' " my sister says. But Audrey didn't say that to me. So when she leaves for work, I investigate the contents of her underwear drawer for what's coming down the pike. Clues to the future: tube girdles with garters and padded bras nested like matryoshka dolls. Slippery underpants. New stockings in flat pink boxes, used ones folded in lace envelopes. Neatly tucked among her underthings are scented heart-shaped sachets. They're satin and the same pink as the top on her cologne bottle. Each sachet has a sash across the front, like a beauty contestant. Instead of "Miss Wyoming" it reads "Schiaparelli."

In real life, I do not see Audrey in anything scantier than a full slip. She is pathologically modest. After she dies, sorting her things in the Florida house, I come across a sheaf of waist-high blindingly white spandex panties, folded once at the equator, stacked like pancakes. They are dense, reinforced, orthopedic undies. When she got terminally sick, she became rail-thin no matter what she ate. She was "cachexic," the medical term for people who can't absorb what they eat. Every part of her was emaciated except her belly. My mother's spleen had exploded, a vicious by-product of lymphoma. I closed the drawer and sold the house.

In 1929, 186 million pairs of undies were manufactured in America, mostly in New York. By 2002, almost all underwear was imported. My UN of Underwear hails from Colombia, Turkey, Macau, China, the Czech Republic, Hong Kong, the Philippines, El Salvador, Myanmar, Bangladesh, Thailand, Indonesia, Vietnam and Taiwan. Hanro of Switzerland's are made in Hungary. The loveliest lace ones come from Haiti. Only one vintage Maidenform bikini I keep for sentimental reasons bears the moving label: "Made in USA, ILGWU, AFL-CIO."

All these affordable little luxuries, so full of promise. They're all that stand between us and nudity. They touch *there*. That's why stores call them *intimates*. No one tells you how to buy them. Once I thought a man I loved wanted me to look virginal. I went to the old B. Altman's, the only department store where you saw nuns shop. In the lingerie department, I asked a salesperson if I could see "the kind of underwear nuns wear."

"What's that?" she said.

"I don't know. What do they buy?"

"They wear the same thing you wear, dear."

I was trying to figure out what men liked. I suspected they cared deeply about visual cues and wanted to get it right. I wound up with waist-high opaque. Larry was disappointed. So for Artie I got see-through red. He wanted me to look like a schoolgirl.

"When you take off your clothes, your personality also undresses and you become quite a different person—more true to yourself and to your real character, more conscious, sometimes more cruel," Schiap writes. I imagine she wears what my grandmothers wear, the French version. That is, until 1940, when it's clear war's inevitable and the Paris of haute luxury vanishes. Men head for the front. Women take their jobs. Servants become scarce. Cloth, food and gas are rationed. These three shortages pervade every aspect of French life. Paris is a city hospitable to bicycles but suddenly eleven million are registered, three times more than the year before. Out of necessity, the jackets in her Cash and Carry Collection have enormous pockets a woman can load with her shopping while keeping her hands free to steer. Simultaneously Schiap reinvents the panty. If the lady of the house must launder her lingerie herself, dress quickly and ride her bike to get places, underpants need to be less complicated and time-consuming. Schiap gets rid of the pleats, length, volume and silk. Because food is scarce, she replaces buttons with elastic at the waist. She uses fabrics that are wrinkle-free and drip-dry. For the first time, French undies don't need to be ironed. They feel good on a bike. Reading this I think, wasn't she a genius to understand that war changes everything, even underpants.

Sometimes on eBay, a pair of Schiaparelli panties turns up. They're what today we call "tap panties." They don't stop at the crease where the thigh meets the pelvis. They look a bit like shorts from vintage girlie calendars, that length. But the fabric is translucent. And something special is going on, something Schiap: chevrons of drip-drip lace or contrasting trim. It's the crotch that dates them. It was thought a woman needed ventilation, that she had to "breathe." The crotch hangs like a hammock. Tampax, invented by Dr. Earle Haas and patented three years before the war, was still looked upon as potentially life-threatening.

My grandmothers' corsets were made of
whalebone, bombazine and elastic.

Wartime panties with a double nylon crotch panel by Schiaparelli.

chapter ten

Gainful Employment

If I have become what I am, I owe it to two distinct things—poverty and Paris. Poverty forced me to work, and Paris gave me a liking for it and courage.

—*Elsa Schiaparelli*

If it weren't for Jo Ann, I'd have been a lawyer.

—*Audrey Volk*

Men hold doors and pull out chairs. They carry luggage. In restaurants, after a brief consultation—"Have you decided what you'd care for?"—men do the ordering:

"My wife would like the sweetbreads and the sole."

They park the car, change chandelier bulbs and tip. They open the wine at home and give the nod to sommeliers in restaurants. They sharpen the knives and carve the roast. Men support their families. They work.

Women work too, but only if they work beside their husbands. Women don't have careers unless they're in show business like Aunt Honey. In the greater world, they can also be teachers, nurses, speech pathologists or, bottom line, salesladies like Aunt Gertie, whose husband gambled away their savings then died of pneumonia.

It is a bona fide tragedy for an adult woman to live without a man, although some poor souls have no choice. A woman who lives without a man—who never married, who is widowed or divorced—is spoken of with pity:

"What a shame. How tragic. She has *nobody.*"

"I was pre-law," Audrey tells my sister. "Then I got pregnant with *you.*"

Jo Ann says nothing even though she went back to school after her kids were born. She raised three while simultaneously getting a master's in social work, setting up practice and patenting four inventions. It doesn't matter to Jo there's a hole in Audrey's logic. Audrey believes her myth. Whether it's true or not, Audrey thinks it's true and that's enough to make Jo the culprit. My sister has diminished her own mother's life by virtue of existing. Because Jo Ann was born, Audrey didn't go to law school. Instead, our mother is the charming hostess of Morgen's West Restaurant, where she is much admired for her style and refinement. She mans the velvet rope, smiling, gracious, exquisitely dressed. Adversity in Audrey's universe takes the form of her firstborn. The unwanted pregnancy that shaped her life. My sister knows this is not fair. That doesn't affect how bad she feels.

Audrey works for free. Working for free has its compensations. She sees Cecil for two and a half hours every day. She's got him to herself until the first customers swing through the doors. Tables will turn over three times before the line begins to wither. But until what I think of as Showtime!, before the wild rumpus starts, Audrey and Cecil sip coffee at a table for two, alone together in a sea of white tablecloths and 230 empty chairs. For twenty minutes, the charming, handsome man everyone wants a piece of is hers. And then it's lunch. Two hours of mania. Top models swan in on the arms of proud designers. Pigeon-breasted manufacturers proudly tap their hankies. Hatcheck girls glow and do a brisk business in cigars and breath purifiers called Choward's Violet. Everybody knows everybody. Everybody checks everybody out. Lunch is party time, Morgen's is packed—a "garment center hang-out," Douglas Martin calls it in *The New York Times,* " . . . a beehive of designers, tycoons, models and hangers-on who waited with showy impatience behind a red velvet rope until a table was open." Working the bronze hook of that red rope, Audrey keeps her eye on everything and everyone, including Dad, who is only too happy to join customers at the bar.

"Did Mom ever get paid?" I ask Aunt Barbara, who was in charge of the rope at Morgen's East.

"We didn't work for money, Patty," she says.

Not that Audrey wants for anything. It may be she prefers being taken care of. Audrey does not aspire to enormous wealth. When I ask, "Are we rich?" she answers, "We're comfortable." She buys what she wants but she isn't reckless. Eventually though, the adjustment to inflation, the new price of certain things, baffles:

"What? Twelve dollars for a tossed salad?"

"Two hundred dollars for an orchestra seat?"

"You spent *what* on those shoes?"

And:

"You gave the delivery boy ten dollars, Patty?"

"Yes, Ma. In Nigeria, he was a brain surgeon."

"Better in your pocket than his."

One of Audrey's favorite things to do is take everyone out for a Ruth's Chris Steak House dinner on her American Express points. She smiles like she's getting away with murder, giddy at the thought of it, steaks for free.

In 1920, Schiap lives on the two cheapest foods you can buy in New York: oysters and ice cream. Her dowry is gone. She's broke. After five miserable years of marriage, de Kerlor has left her. She is twenty-nine when she gives birth alone. Because the baby gurgles, Schiap nicknames her "Gogo." Countess Maria Luisa Yvonne Radha de Wendt de Kerlor sleeps in an orange crate in a rented room in Greenwich Village. I read about Schiap's "gnawing, black hunger" and don't understand. Her childhood is so much like mine—an intact family, lessons, books, museums, loving caretakers—and she's starving?

When my father increases my allowance to a dollar, I start saving.

Patty's Budget

45 cents—ham sandwich at Schrafft's
5 cents—Coke
10 cents—tip
25 cents—movie
5 cents—Jujubes

I put 10 cents away every week. When I see my grandfather, he reaches into his pocket, stirs his change, and says, "Are you broke?"

"No," I can honestly say.

To help her impoverished daughter, Signora Schiaparelli ships her late husband's prized gold-coin collection to New York. Schiap sells it and stretches the proceeds as long as she can. But then she is moneyless again until, by chance, she has a bit of pure luck: "One night I went for a walk and a piece of paper fluttered at my feet. I picked it up. It was a twenty dollar bill." She treats herself to a steak dinner and the next day, with what's left of the twenty, buys "two small objects" in a pawnbroker's shop downtown. She sells them uptown for a profit. She chops off her hair and sets out to find work. But women of her class are not trained to do anything. Selling imported French dresses for a friend, Schiap discovers that rich New York women *prefer* sailing to Paris to shop for their clothes. She grabs whatever job is offered—reading tickertapes on Wall Street, typing letters for a Russian relief fund. Stieglitz gets her stand-in work on a movie project in New Jersey. All day Schiap poses under blazing lights until she goes temporarily blind.

And then she gets lucky a second time: A friend invites her to Paris. The woman wants a quick French divorce and Schiap is fluent in French. In Paris, Schiap decides she'd like a divorce too. To pay for it, she becomes a "picker," shopping Paris flea markets for an antiques dealer. Schiap has "an eye." Since she can't afford a dressmaker and she can't sew, she cobbles her clothes, "my head full of wild ideas." She finesses what she can't engineer under shawls, scarves and fur. She works up sketches and makes appointments with couturiers. At the House of Maggy Rouff, she is told, "You would do better to plant potatoes than to try to make dresses. You have no talent or *métier.*"

What is it about Elsa Schiaparelli? Strangers have faith in her. They can't wait to help her. In 1925, a wealthy American admires Schiap's style and backs her in a tiny dress shop, "Madame Lambal," on rue Saint-Honoré. The press raves about Schiap's "individuality." Soon she has her own place thanks to a silent partner. She insists Monsieur Kahn set her up on the most fashionable street in the world. At 4, rue de la Paix the attic is so small, no chairs or changing rooms can fit. The heat doesn't work. A terrier, brought in to keep the rats at bay, is terrified of rats. Customers must climb six flights of stairs. They're happy to.

And then one day, walking down the rue de l'Université, Schiap notices a woman wearing a sweater knit in a look she calls "steady." She tracks down the knitter. An Armenian refugee named Aroosiag Mikaelian explains how the complicated stitch, using two different colors of wool, works.

"If I make a design will you try to copy it?" Schiap asks.

"Mike" agrees to try.

"So I draw a large butterfly bow in front, like a scarf round the neck—the primitive drawing of a child in prehistoric times. The poor darling, not at all disturbed by such a mad idea, struggled to work it out. Indeed, this was something I was to discover throughout my career, that people would always follow my ideas enthusiastically, and try without discussion to do what I told them." (Schiap's friend Dalí calls this effect "paranoiac delirium." He too believes he can bend people to his will and make them act out his ideas.)

Schiap folds her love of Surrealism into the design.

The pullover sports an ecru butterfly bow and deep cuffs knitted right into the sweater.

On her third try, Mike gets it right.

What happens next makes Schiaparelli world-famous: She's invited to a fashion luncheon for American buyers at the Ritz. She times herself to get there late. Everyone is already seated when Schiap makes her entrance in the sweater. There is a collective gasp as she wends her way to her table. Lord & Taylor orders forty on the spot. American *Vogue* calls the surreal sweater "an artistic masterpiece." The House of Schiaparelli is launched. A crew of Armenian knitters knit for Schiap full-time. The sweaters touch a nerve. What is in the air for art is in the air for fashion.

Schiap designs more surreal sweaters with trompe-l'oeil designs—men's ties, crossword puzzles, tattoos—knitted into them. She makes a hat with the crenellations of a brain. She collaborates with Dalí on La Lanterne, an evening bag that has a tiny battery-operated street lamp on the outside. She asks the artist Jean Dunand to adopt an airbrush technique from the automobile industry and paint surreal folds on a white evening gown. Visiting Copenhagen, Schiap notices women in the fish market wear hats made out of newspapers. She pastes together a collage of her newspaper reviews, has it printed on silk, then makes shirts and scarves out of it. She introduces the first jumpsuit, the wrap dress and paper clothes. During the day, for work, her Transformable Dress grazes the knees. For evening, a ribbon is pulled and the dress descends into a floor-length evening gown. She invents foldable eyeglasses and wins patent after patent. Schiap is the first designer to have people pay to publicize her name. In 1929, she buys out Monsieur Kahn and becomes the sole owner of "Schiaparelli." (Chanel will never own more than 20 percent of "Chanel.") Her umbrellas slip into scabbards. Her gloves have gold talons. She designs costumes for thirty movies and twenty-nine plays. Joan Crawford falls for Schiap's tray shoulders. Marlene Dietrich sprouts her black rooster "wings." *Vogue* calls Schiap a "clothes carpenter." Jean Cocteau says she is "a young demon who tempts women, who leads the mad carnival in a burst of laughter." He refers to her atelier as "a devil's laboratory." *Harper's Bazaar* calls the House of Schiaparelli "The House of Ideas." She opens a tiny shop next to 21, place Vendôme. She invents the word "boutique" from the French word *bouticle,* a store on the first floor of a business establishment. For the first time, French women can buy clothes on the spot, *prêt-à-porter,* and not wait for them to be custom-made. Janet Flanner (the American "Letter from Paris" correspondent known as "Genet") profiles Schiap in *The New Yorker:* "A dress from Schiaparelli ranks like a modern canvas."

She brings new materials to couture: latex, straw, rubber, cork, mattress ticking, Rhodophane. She designs the first shoulder bag for women, the Bandolier, based on a French railway guard's bag. *Time* magazine says, "Mme. Schiaparelli is the one to whom the word 'genius' is applied most often." Dresses flaunt her "Telegram Print" with a message: ALL IS WELL. MOTHER-IN-LAW IN TERRIBLE SHAPE. After King Edward abdicates the throne so he can marry the twice-divorced Wallis Simpson, Mrs. Simpson buys eighteen Schiaparellis for her honeymoon, including the Lobster Dress, painted by Dalí. The dress is a phallic joke. The predatory claws fall between the legs. The Duchess of Windsor doesn't get it. She believes the dress will show the world she has a sense of humor.

By 1934, Schiap is the most famous couturier in the world. My dazzling mother could have been anything. What stopped her? Cecil owns a restaurant, holds several patents, and sculpts and paints on the side. Jo has a busy practice and she's an inventor too. I'm a writer. Once when the four of us are having dinner together, Audrey says: "You know what my job is here? You know what is expected?"

We wait for her answer.

She looks at each of us, going from Cecil to Jo Ann to me. Then she claps.

The sweater that launched the House of Schiaparelli.

Wallis Simpson in the Lobster Dress. She didn't get the joke.

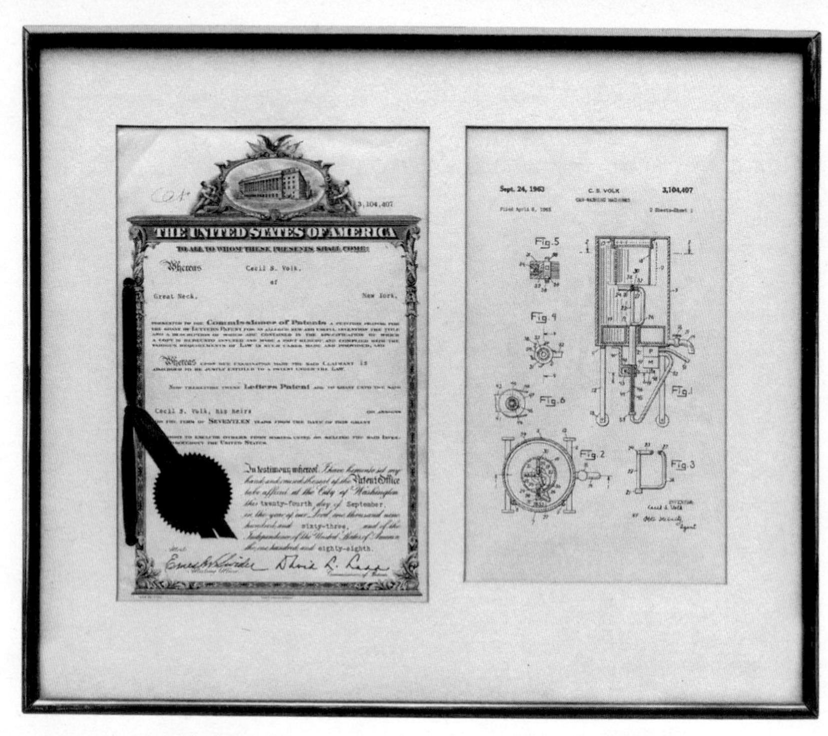

3,104,407

THE UNITED STATES OF AMERICA

TO ALL TO WHOM THESE PRESENTS SHALL COME:

Whereas Cecil S. Volk, of Great Neck, New York,

Commissioner of Patents

Whereas

Letters Patent

Cecil S. Volk, his heirs

SEVENTEEN

In testimony whereof I have hereunto set my hand and caused the seal of the Patent Office to be affixed at the City of Washington this twenty-fourth day of September, in the year of our Lord one thousand nine hundred and sixty-three, and of the Independence of the United States of America the one hundred and eighty-eighth.

Sept. 24, 1963 C. S. VOLK 3,104,407

Dad believed his patent for the double-sided garbage-can brush was stolen by the car wash industry.

The Five Vices by Cecil Sussman Volk. (One vice was painted over.)

chapter eleven

The Vicissitudes of Beauty

> There are only two aunts and one uncle remaining and I am now a grandmother of five but at any gathering of the clan, I can still hear the soft tones of my elders saying, "Look at her."
>
> —*Audrey Volk (journal entry)*

> To have a face covered with flowers like a heavenly garden would indeed be a wonderful thing! And if she could make flowers sprout all over her face, she would be the only woman of her kind in the whole world.
>
> —*Elsa Schiaparelli*

A man stops Audrey in the playground:

"Excuse, please?"

Vuk Vuchinich, the *Time* magazine cover artist, is looking for faces.

"Please, miss. You may to let me draw you, yes?"

Audrey's used to it. On vacations, the hotel's portrait artist cajoles her into sitting for free. Guests hover in the lobby as my mother is immortalized in Las Brisas, the Ocean Club and Mauna Kea. Photos are turned into paintings. Paintings are transferred to porcelain.

"She looks just like Lana Turner!" people say.

The Lana Turner opposition bristles. "She most certainly does not! She's the spitting image of Grace Kelly."

They take sides.

Every woman who isn't beautiful wonders at some moment in her life what life would have been like had she been beautiful. I have friends who never had to work. I call their existence "The Curse of Inherited Wealth." Extreme beauty is inherited wealth. But what chance does a beautiful woman have? To be constantly admired for something she can't take credit for, something that every day disappears a little bit more. Yet beauty matters. According to Audrey, beauty is a woman's greatest asset, the most valuable thing a woman can have. She makes this clear. After running into an acquaintance, as soon as she's out of earshot, Audrey comments first on how that person looks:

"She used to be so pretty."

"Poor thing. You can't hide that kind of skin."

And the one that terrifies: "Tsk, tsk. Isn't it a shame? She's lost her looks."

Every September, when she escorts me on the opening day of school, I check, panicky, to make sure my mother is the youngest and most beautiful. She is.

Sundays, the one day a week a restaurant man gets to breakfast with his family, Cecil flails his napkin in his lap, leans in and says: "Girls, isn't your mother the most beautiful woman in the world?"

Beauty is work. Even if, like Audrey, you're born beautiful, beauty requires constant vigilance. A pimple foments an emergency trip to the dermatologist. Feet are maintained by a visiting chiropodist. A dignified woman named Bea Irsa, carrying a wicker suitcase that contains a hot plate, makes house calls. Behind Audrey's closed door, Mrs. Irsa, who sees more of my mother than I ever will, waxes away unwanted hair.

Maintenance of fingernails, hairdo and body tone takes place outside the home. One of Audrey's exercise instructors, Marian McGlone, teaches her a condensed form of calisthenics she performs every morning when her feet hit the floor. They're brutal but take just seven minutes.

Beauty is not a free ride. Age is the enemy. Once it is established you are beautiful, people try to find reasons you're not. Later, Audrey will refuse to celebrate her birthday. She will refuse to acknowledge her anniversary too. She moves to a new town and no one knows how old she is. If someone knows you married at eighteen and you're celebrating your fiftieth anniversary, how hard is it to do the math?

In her forties, although she is still the Most Beautiful Woman in the World, Audrey begins taking more pains with her makeup. She issues a puzzling edict: "I can no longer wear black." Passing the hall mirror, she stops, presses her palms against her cheeks and pulls. She gleans names from *Vogue* and *Harper's Bazaar.* She queries her hairdresser. Mr. Paris knows scars firsthand, knows who does good "work." Hiding behind dark glasses and a scarf, my mother makes the rounds of New York's leading plastic surgeons. The Most

Beautiful Woman in the World is considering a face-lift. To us, Audrey is as flawless as ever. Why would she tamper with that face? But she sees things we don't. And she's not happy about it. Her face has become her adversary. She weighs her options, performing due diligence, taking into account each doctor's reputation, the look of the office, his personality and grooming, what he's wearing, the refinement of his staff, what he thinks she "needs," what hospital he's affiliated with, where he trained, whether he's board-certified, if he teaches, whether he strikes her as discreet, does he naïvely try the kiss of death—the "hard sell"?—how many diplomas and certificates hang on his wall and how tastefully they're framed and arranged. She will be placing her face in the hands of a stranger.

After completing her research, she commits to Dr. Smith. One question remains: Should the face-lift be just her face, or should it also involve her neck? My father, my sister and I are canvassed for opinions. We sit around the dining table and discuss Audrey's neck. Anything that concerns Audrey is important and newsworthy: a new filling in a tooth, replating the silver ice bucket, a haircut or new shoes. The upside of doing the neck will be a tightening or firming. The downside, there is no way to avoid a two-inch scar on the ventral side of her chin. My mother doesn't have any scars anywhere except for a fading ovoid smallpox vaccination on her upper left arm, and a tiny deformity on her right big toe from an ingrown nail. There is also the ghost of a line—but it's almost invisible, you have to look for it—in the natural folds of her neck where Dr. Max Som excised a branchial cleft cyst (an ontogenic gestational gill). All of us feel rotten her beauty must bear the burden of any scars at all. She is too perfect for imperfection.

After the third family neck meeting, a strange thing happens. Quite suddenly, out of nowhere, I notice empty skin beneath Audrey's chin. It looks soft. It's barely there. You couldn't fit a grape in it. Who knows? Maybe she would be better off without it. So what if there's a little scar? Who sees the underside of your chin? You have to throw your head back and laugh like a madman, which is not the kind of thing Audrey does. In the end, Audrey elects to keep the pouch. No matter what her decision is, we're behind it. We want her to be happy.

The morning of the surgery, we arrive at the hospital at seven. We wait with Audrey in the dark wood-paneled room she will occupy during her stay. The doctor has scheduled her for eight. All of us are pleased she is his second patient of the day. He will have warmed up, but not be tired. At seven-thirty a nurse administers a drip to make Audrey drowsy. But something goes wrong. The operation is postponed. The doctor has an emergency. Audrey is rescheduled for eleven and given more medicine to relax. Then something goes wrong again. We bring in lunch from the local deli and discuss what kind of emergency a plastic surgeon could have. A movie star went through a windshield? The mayor broke his nose? Nurses sweep in and give her medicine to keep calm. The surgery is postponed again and again. We sit around her bed, my father and I, all day, watching her doze, her beautiful face in drugged repose as shadows grow on the wall. She is rolled into the operating room at six. When she comes downstairs two hours later, Audrey is swathed like the Invisible Man.

She spends three nights in the hospital, then Cecil drives her home. When the black-and-blues disappear and the swelling subsides, she is taut and still beautiful. But she's different. It's hard to pinpoint the changes between her new face and the original. She looks like a police sketch of herself. There's more than a resemblance. I'd recognize her, anybody who knew her old face would. But it's a different face. It's not the face I know. I can't remember her real face. I have to look at old photo albums to see the face I love.

Later, much later, she confides that the doctor, exhausted after a full day in the OR, severed a nerve on one side of her mouth. She doesn't want anyone to know, especially Dad. But every time Audrey is with people, she has to compensate, a conscious act to elevate one side of her mouth. She exerts herself into symmetry. And I, student of her beauty, don't know this for thirty years, that's how well she manages it. Only when she becomes so sick she doesn't have the strength to hoist her left *levator labii superioris alaeque nasi* muscle do I catch the droop. She has two more face-lifts before she dies, but the smile is unfixable. Once you sever the *levator labii superioris alaeque nasi* nerve, that's it.

Schiap will never be pretty like her sister, Beatrice. Both of her cheeks are sprayed with moles. Her left cheek is worse, eleven raised ones. She hates to have her picture taken. "Schiap was an ugly child as standards go," she writes. "Her mother began making disparaging remarks about her looks. She was always being told she was as ugly as her sister was beautiful." The astronomer Giovanni Schiaparelli—discoverer of the Canals of Mars, and director of Milan's

Brera Observatory—tells his niece that, no, she isn't *bruta.* "He liked me because he used to say I was born with the constellation of the Great Bear on my cheek. They were, of course, beauty spots." Seven of the moles scattered over her left cheek loosely form the Big Dipper, the central part of Ursa Major. Uncle Giovanni invites Elsa to his observatory so she can look through his telescope and see her cheek in the sky. From then on she sees her face a different way. She is convinced her moles are lucky. Years later, she uses the Big Dipper repeatedly in her collections, embroidering it, printing it on fabric. She asks Cartier to make her a Big Dipper brooch using diamonds for the stars, and wears it, echoing her moles.

"Schiap still considered her sister much better looking than herself and this made her increasingly shy." The little girl invents a way to make herself prettier than Beatrice. What is more beautiful than flowers? What if she can get flowers to grow on her face? If flowers are beautiful, her face will be beautiful. She convinces the gardener to give her seeds from her favorites: nasturtiums, poppies and morning glories. She closes the door to the bathroom and studies her face in the mirror. She pushes the seeds up her nose as far as they'll go. She plants her ears and her mouth. She waits for her face to burst into bloom. Once her face is covered with flowers, she will be more beautiful than her sister.

That evening at dinner, something is wrong. Elsa barely touches her food. She's having trouble breathing. Signora Schiaparelli dispatches a servant to the doctor's house. The seeds are extracted except for one that has worked its way into her sinus, discovered at a later date.

Face planting marks Schiap's first foray into Surrealism.

Twenty years later, does she tell her good friend Salvador Dalí about it? One of her favorite paintings—Dalí gives it to her—is his *Necrophiliac Springtime.* In the painting, a beautifully gowned woman has a bouquet for a head.

No matter how famous Schiap becomes, throughout her life she returns to flowers to telegraph beauty. The firm of Lesage beads them onto sweaters, jackets and gowns. Silk flowers grow out of necklines, waistbands and hats. Sometimes flowers are the hat in its entirety. Pockets on summer dresses are printed with seed packets. Women pluck the glass nosegay from the Shocking perfume presentation and wear it as a brooch, so Schiap has it made into a brooch.

As an adult, Schiap's long face presents with hooded eyes, a high domed forehead and a voluptuous lower lip. Her upper lip is short. Her brown eyes turn down at the corners and the skin around them is sunken and dark. She knows she's not pretty. She's referred to as a *jolie-laide.* Beautiful-ugly women are not conventionally good-looking. Their faces are idiosyncratic, off-kilter, ill-proportioned. But something makes them *jolie* too. It's a combination of attitude and style. They groom themselves impeccably and dress with imagination. They have flawless carriage and hold themselves as if they are in fact beauties. When a *jolie-laide* enters a room, heads turn. *Jolie-laides* compel. They are referred to as "striking." "Striking" is a way of saying "not beautiful but worthy of attention." Famous *jolie-laides* are Diana Vreeland, Anjelica Huston and the Duchess of Windsor.

In Paris in the 1920s, it is said that you haven't arrived until your portrait has been taken by Man Ray. "To be done by Man Ray means that you were rated as somebody," said Sylvia Beach, the expatriate bookseller and publisher of

James Joyce's *Ulysses*. Schiap trusts him. She poses for many photos, and most of the time he airbrushes her Big Dipper out. In his 1932 surreal *Self-Portrait with Camera,* Man Ray reveals that he too had a cheek speckled with moles. He leaves his in.

There are advantages to not being a great beauty. Beauty fades and the only thing sadder than losing it is trying to keep it. If you are not beautiful, something more lasting gets to be the coin of your realm. Schiap will never suffer the fate of her earlier neighbor on the place Vendôme, the outrageously beautiful Countess di Castiglione, cousin of Cavour, mistress of Napoleon III. As she grew older and less beautiful, Castiglione covered her mirrors and painted her rooms black. She waited until nightfall to go for a walk. According to Schiap, Castiglione "mourned in solitude the fatal passing of a nearly divine beauty."

Audrey would have known what to do. If she could have gotten her hands on Schiap, she'd have said: "Find an excellent dermatologist, darling. Have those moles removed. No one will miss them. And your hairdresser? He isn't doing you any favors. See an orthodontist and get a retainer. Push that overbite back. Above all, this is very important, concealer for under your eyes. And darling, don't be stingy."

Vuk Vuchinich's portrait of the Yugoslavian partisan
Draža Mihailović and his portrait of Audrey Volk.

Audrey in oil. Audrey in hotel-lobby pastel. Did she look more like Lana Turner or Grace Kelly?

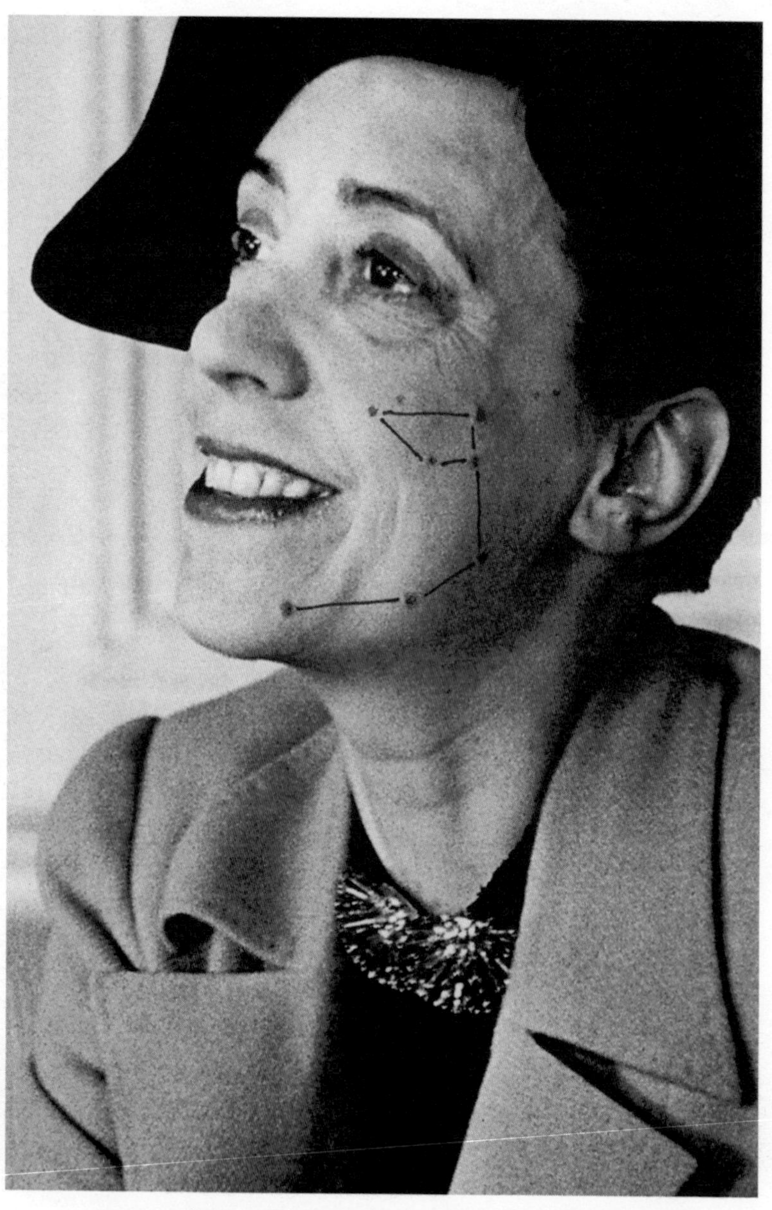

Schiap's uncle, a world-famous astronomer, told her that the "beauty spots" on her face formed the Big Dipper.

Schiap, accompanied by her friend and collaborator Salvador Dalí, wears her diamond Big Dipper brooch to the races.

Necrophiliac Springtime, a gift to Schiap from Salvador Dalí in 1936. The woman's head is made entirely of flowers.

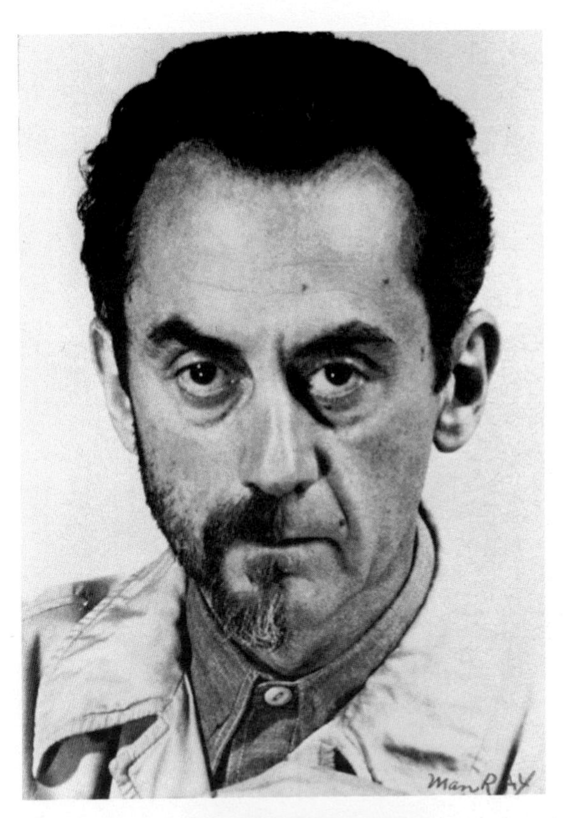

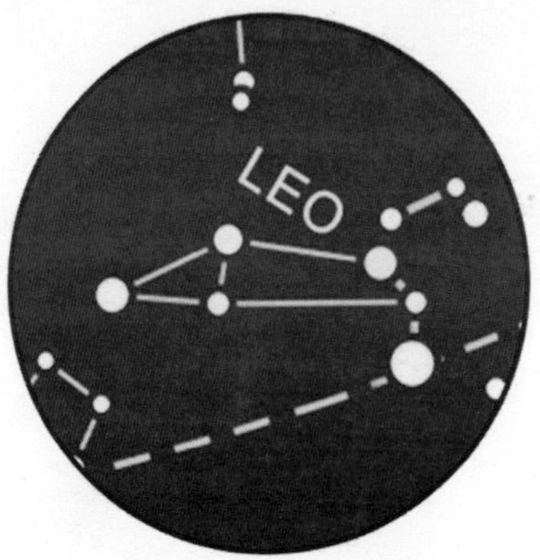

Man Ray's "beauty spots" formed the constellation of Leo.
He retouched Schiap's portraits, but not his own.

The famous beauty the Countess di Castiglione
once lived on the place Vendôme.
Schiap's surreal Profile Hat has a jeweled eyebrow.

I gave this hand mirror to my mother on her birthday. The engraving reads: "For the Most Beautiful Woman in the World 1.21.90."

chapter twelve

Improving the Mind

The fact that I was obliged to learn things I did not care about, and curb my imagination, revolted me. Mathematics was my worst subject, and I was invariably at the bottom of my class. I could not grasp figures, and thus it has always been with me.

—*Elsa Schiaparelli*

I returned to school that January, prepared for the anomaly of becoming an average student. No longer would I stand with chalk in my hand at the blackboard, demonstrating the solution to a problem. Nor would my arm be waving like a banner over the heads of my classmates, so that my voice could be heard first in response to the teacher's question. I accepted the role graciously and with a light heart, happy to abandon the responsibilities of "stardom."

—*Audrey Volk (journal entry)*

Every September Audrey Morgen's new teachers steel themselves for the worst.

"Are you Robert Morgen's sister?"

But Audrey is a model of decorum. Trusty messenger to the principal's office, keeper of the Hall Pass, honored fire-drill monitor. The prettiest, the smartest. The only girl in an extended family with six male first cousins, attention is lavished. Expectations reach the stratosphere. The goal is perfection. Flawless straight-A report cards are brandished at the dinner table. Year after year, Audrey reigns at the top of her class. In prewar New York the prevailing wisdom is: If a child does remarkably well, it's in that child's best interest to skip a grade. Everyone agrees: Intellectual nourishment transcends the value of social adjustment. Understimulating a child is a crime. As a result, girls and boys graduate high school at twelve and toddle off to college.

In June, on the last day of public school, Polly leans out her kitchen window. Waving Audrey's report card, she shouts to the other kitchen windows on the airshaft, "Audrey skipped *again*!" Thus my mother finds herself, one September, to be eleven in the ninth grade. Her classmates are fifteen.

"I had no idea what the teachers were talking about in history." She shakes her head. "I was completely lost. No one spoke to me. The older girls wore grown-up clothes and silk stockings clipped to their garter belts. I was still in cotton lisles."

Math makes no sense either. "It was as if the teacher were speaking a foreign language."

Audrey is terrified. "My little world was turned upside

down. Before the first report card was due, I knew I had to face shattering the family's dream." One night she bolts up in bed and howls. Polly and Herman rush in.

Audrey wails out her fear of failure.

Do the words "resort" and "restore" have the same origin? The next morning, Polly whisks her little girl away to a resort in Lakewood, New Jersey. "It was famous for restoring visitors to the best of health," Audrey's journal reads. "This was accomplished by walking around the lake and inhaling aromatic, pine-scented air. Mother and I walked and walked but I still didn't know the missed history, geography and grammar."

Back home, the family convenes. A decision is made. Audrey will sit out the rest of the term and enter a new school in a new grade in January. She spends the weeks reading biographies, "nursing my wounded spirit in the company of famous scientists, artists, writers and theatrical personalities." She begins to reassemble. After Christmas break, she enters the Calhoun School in the eighth grade.

Joining a class midterm, a class of older children who have grown up together since kindergarten, Audrey is a guaranteed outsider. She's the new girl. Her smartness and prettiness work against her. Who wants to be friends with someone smarter and prettier? She invites classmates to her father's restaurants. She tries to make movie dates for Saturdays. When nothing works, Audrey devises a plan. She studies Edith, the most popular girl, then copies her. Like Edith, Audrey compliments people and stops gossiping. Like Edith, Audrey smiles. Eating lunch alone, she smiles. Last one chosen for a team, she smiles. Audrey laughs without mercy and forces herself to look like the happiest girl in the world. One day, walking home after school, Edith invites her to play acey-deucey. Soon Audrey is having Chinese food with Gladys upstairs on Broadway and watching double features with Rhea and Edna. Naomi becomes her partner in crime. Together they sneak into Wednesday matinees after school. Two starstruck girls become "second-acters," scouting empty seats in the theater as the audience thins after intermission. They see the last two acts of every Broadway show for free. When their parents ask them where they've been, Audrey and Naomi say, "Glee Club."

For the rest of her life Audrey maintains an outward aura of happiness. "If you act a certain way," she paraphrases William James, "you become that way." She creates a persona designed to inspire envy. This makes her feel enviable. "I always think everything I have is the best," she likes to say. Her dentist is the best. Her husband is the best. Her apartment is the best. The woman who decorates her apartment is the best, as is the Syrie Maugham sofa this best decorator persuades her to buy. Her manicurist and her hair colorist are the best. Though her daughters could use a little work, when presented to the outside world they're the best too. Her grandchildren, who go to the best schools, say the best, most quotable things.

After a big party (she throws the best parties, with the best food and the best conversation), I help my mother fold her freshly laundered napkins. She teaches me the best way to "iron" drip-drys: You lay the napkin flat on top of the dryer and smooth it with the side of your palm. Then you fold it in half, and smooth it again using elbow grease on the crease. The napkins look perfectly ironed.

When I leave my job to write full-time, Audrey decides

she'd like to be a writer too. A spiral-bound journal becomes her constant companion. She takes adult-education classes in nonfiction at the local high school. She joins a group led by a woman who teaches in her home. Audrey hurls herself into her craft. She glows with it. One of her essays knocks the class out. Everyone agrees how good it is. Lucille, the harshest critic, takes Audrey aside and says, "I was moved by your piece." The essay is about Audrey's early adventures sneaking into second acts with Naomi and the time they slipped backstage and met Burgess Meredith.

"I think this is publishable," the teacher says.

Thrilled and encouraged, Audrey submits her essay to *Playbill.* Our family is in a state of happy agitation. Audrey is poised to become a professional essayist. We wait for her to receive her first acceptance letter. My mother, a published author. When people ask her what she does, she'll be able to say, "I'm a writer." We imagine all the theatergoers who will read her brilliant piece before the curtain goes up. Every person for one month who sees a Broadway show will know Audrey Volk is a writer. Perhaps there will be a little biography at the bottom of the article: *Audrey Volk, hostess of Morgen's West, has been attending theater since the age of* 6. Or: *Audrey Morgen Volk was born in New York and is a full-time writer.*

A week goes by. Then two. The class presses Audrey to call *Playbill.* She leaves a message. Two more weeks go by. She calls again. Lucille urges her to say, "I'm going to have to withdraw the piece for consideration if I don't hear back from you." Everyone in class is astonished by how rude *Playbill* is. Someone suggests she ignore the rule about only submitting a piece to one publication at a time. Audrey calls again and leaves another message. This one reminds *Playbill* that she went to the trouble of including an SASE with her submission. A week later, a letter arrives. The house organ of New York's theater world would prefer not to encourage second-acters.

When Audrey and Cecil begin contemplating a move to Florida, my mother is terrified that, without her lifelong friends, her work, without Broadway, museums and the opera, she'll feel marginalized. She does not want a shrink-wrapped life of club committees and canasta. Two years prior to departure, she makes a life-changing decision. She embarks on the time-honored adventure people take when they want to change their lives: She goes back to school in earnest and prepares herself for a new career. This time Audrey decides to try her older daughter's profession. She hires a tutor to help her study for the GREs. Her scores are good enough for her to get into graduate school. She chooses Hofstra College because they give her the most credits for life experience. Before leaving New York, Audrey earns her graduate degree in family counseling and social work. My sister, a practicing therapist, refers to Audrey's M.S.W. as "The License to Kill."

The first place she interviews in Florida, Audrey's hired. She joins a private practice where she will see clients who can't afford the more established therapists. She'll earn 50 percent of the fee per session—the rest goes to the group—but she'll have supervision, on-the-job training. Audrey dives into her work. She loves learning. She takes copious notes on clients and turns her new library into an office. She gets a computer and a printer and has her first big patient success with a florist. He works for the shop that supplies the centerpieces for Mar-a-Lago, the Marjorie Merriweather

Post estate then owned by Donald Trump. The young man is being kept by an older man. He is miserable but can't afford to live on his own.

"What makes you happy?" Audrey asks him.

"Arranging flowers."

"Are you good at it?"

"Very."

"The next time you go to Mar-a-Lago, why don't you ask Ivana Trump if you could have a chance to do a party for her? Tell her you'll do her flowers free the first time."

The patient follows Audrey's instructions. Ivana is delighted by his work. He is hired. He becomes a huge success in Palm Beach and gets his own apartment.

"Do you like being a therapist?" I ask my mother.

She thinks before answering. "I don't like treating the sociopaths," she says.

"Who do you like to treat?"

"I always thought my patients would be women my age who were having a little trouble with their husbands."

Purely out of curiosity I ask her: "Did you ever think of divorcing Dad?"

My mother answers with great care: "I may have thought of leaving him once, getting away for a while. But I never considered divorcing him. That would be out of the question."

I think of Audrey and Cecil as Harlequin shrimp. A vulnerable breed, they depend on each other, hunting together and mating for life.

When we're alone, I ask Cecil if he ever thought of divorcing Audrey.

"Never!" he says, puzzled I could ask such a thing.

It's comforting to read that at La Scuola di Signorina Arnoletto, Elsa spends most of her time like I do in school: staring out the window. My view is light shifting on the gray façade of 465 West End Avenue. Elsa gazes at the voluptuous bronze naiads on Rutelli's Fontana dell'Acqua Marcia in the Piazza delle Terme.

Freud called daydreaming infantile and neurotic. (He created a brand-new science and he didn't daydream?) However, researchers have discovered that tuning out can be useful. According to recent experiments reported by John Tierney in *The New York Times,* daydreaming "fosters creativity and helps you solve problems." But in school it hardly helps. Schiap and I do miserably. Math, in particular, is torture. We suffer from numbing dyscalculia, the inability to solve even the most basic math problems. It's a form of brain dysfunction, not affecting general intelligence, that afflicts 7 percent of the population. I listen to the teacher, I write things down, I try, but it slips away like the dregs of a dream. The high point of my school day is racing home for lunch and watching *Love of Life* and *Search for Tomorrow* while eating a spectacular sandwich made by Mattie: ham on rye with mayo and mustard and a crunchy chiffonade of iceberg lettuce, or gooey chopped egg, still warm, with burnt bacon and Russian dressing on toast.

Elsa has to eat the school lunch, and it's nothing like the Roman food Rosa the cook makes at the Palazzo Corsini. At school she's forced to down watery yellow soup. She begs her mother to call and complain. The signora shakes her head.

The food can't possibly be as bad as her melodramatic daughter says it is.

"Per favore, Papa," she pleads with her father to intervene. But the Schiaparellis are indivisible. Like Audrey and Cecil, they're a united front.

Celestino adores both of his daughters but worries less about Beatrice. Beatrice is devout, quiet and beautiful and will have many suitors to choose from. It is Elsa, headstrong and volatile, moody and questioning, Elsa, who will never be beautiful, who must understand that she has a say in her fate. The child is clever, even if she does not do well in school. That evening, before dinner, Celestino takes his disappointed daughter by the hand. They go for a walk. They climb a hill. When they reach the top, there is a church. On the roof of the church, there is a *campanile.* Standing beneath the bell, they catch their breath. After resting a bit, Celestino leans over the parapet.

"Look," he calls to his daughter, pointing to the square below. Twisting streets radiate out from the piazza like tentacles.

"Do you see, *carissima,*" Celestino says, "there is more than one way to the square. Life is like that, Elsa. If you can't reach your destination by one road, try another."

The next day at school, while no one is watching, Elsa pours the thin soup into a jar. Back home, as she does every day, she sneaks into the kitchen to play with the servants and nibble their rough bread. Then she starts to work on Rosa. She pleads, she begs. Finally, she persuades the cook to serve the school soup to her mother at dinner.

Seated around the family table in the Palazzo Corsini, beneath the frescoed ceiling, surrounded by ancient tapestries, the first course arrives. Maria-Luisa dips her spoon into her soup. She brings it to her lips. Her eyes widen.

"Has the cook gone mad?"

Elsa confesses. She is not punished. From that day on every morning Rosa packs two baskets of food, one for Elsa, one for Beatrice, to take to school. There is always more than one way to the center of the square.

The schooling of a Roman girl of privilege does not include college. In a few years, Elsa will sneak into the University of Rome and study philosophy. She will fall in love with Spinoza. For the rest of her life she'll continue to study. She reads in her library on the rue de Berri, surrounded by books—books on the floor, books on chairs, books piled up to the ceiling. Trussed in her turban, wearing satin evening pajamas and gold platform sandals, curled on a velvet bergère, she reads long into the night, slowly turning pages and sipping the drink she invented, Pink Vodka.

And all three of us, my mother, Schiaparelli and I, wind up loving school once we're older, once we don't have to cope with geometry and memorize dates. It turns out we are all excellent students, just as long we can study what we want.

Attendance and Punctuality

	Oct. 31 / Mar. 15	Dec. 15 / May 15	Jan. 31 / Jun. 30	
ABSENT	4	4	8	4
LATE	0	0	0	0

First Report

In view of this pupil's ability, he (she)
1. Is doing very well
2. Is doing satisfactory work ✓
3. Could do better
4. Shows little effort

I have read this report
Parent's Signature Audrey Volk

Second Report

In view of this pupil's ability, he (she)
1. Is doing very well ✓
2. Is doing satisfactory work
3. Could do better
4. Shows little effort

I have read this report
Parent's Signature Audrey Volk

Third Report

In view of this pupil's ability, he (she)
1. Is doing very well ✓
2. Is doing satisfactory work ✓ #
3. Could do better
4. Shows little effort

I have read this report
Parent's Signature Audrey Volk

Class next term..................

43

77-6715 (Kg-1B) 170M-2-47

P. S. 9 Borough Man.

Board of Education

Pro. to 2-1 City of New York
Room 311
Teacher Miss Sussman

Report Card

Term beginning Sept 1949

Name Patricia Volk

Class 1-1 Room 209

Teacher E S Plesser

TO PARENTS:

The school is trying to aid the growth of your child in scholarship, in health habits and in character. To get the best results, inside and outside school, your help is needed.

The principal and the teacher will be pleased to talk matters over with you.

NAME Patricia Volk

In the development of these traits, the home shares responsibility with the school.

TRAINING IN PERSONALITY	Oct. 31 / Mar. 15	Dec. 15 / May 15	Jan. 31 / Jun. 30	
GOOD PERSONAL HABITS These include:				
Posture				
Sitting correctly	S	S	S	S
Standing correctly	S	S	S	S
Walking correctly	S	S	S	S
Cleanliness				
Keeping hands, nails, face and teeth clean	S	S	S	S
Keeping hands and materials away from mouth	S	S	S	S
Using a handkerchief	S	S	S	S
Covering mouth when coughing	S	S	S	S
Keeping clothing clean	S	S	S	S
Ability to dress alone	S	S	S	S
GOOD SOCIAL HABITS These include:				
Working and playing well with others	S	S	S	S
Responding to signals promptly	S	S	S	S
Respecting the rights of others	S	S	S	S

Scholarship	Oct. 31 / Mar. 15	Dec. 15 / May 15	Jan. 31 / Jun. 30	
GOOD WORK HABITS These include:				
Working alone	S	S	S	S
Doing purposeful work	I	S	S	S
Finishing work	S	S	S	S
EVIDENCES OF GROWTH IN:				
Ability to express himself	S	S	S	S
Learning to read	I	S	S	S
Speaking clearly	S	S	S	S
Behavior	A	✓	✓	✓
Very creative child.		✓	✓	
greatly improved in read.				✓

S—Satisfactory

U—Unsatisfactory

I—Improvement shown

First P.S. 9 report card. I learned to read but could only write mirror-writing.

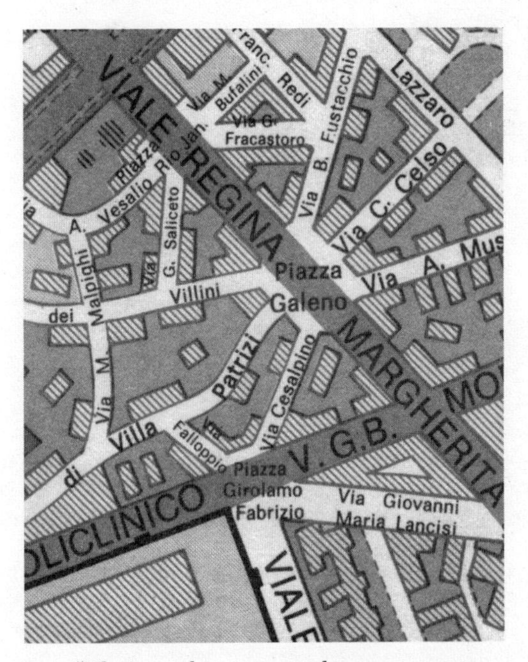

"There is always more than one way
to the center of the square."

Audrey Volk March 29, 1982

Green Velvet

The words "green velvet" conjure up vivid scenes from various stages of my life. The first took place when I was five years old. My mother sewed beautifully and made most of my clothes. One day she purchased a few yards of lovely green silk velvet with which to make me a matching hat and coat for winter. After many fittings and decisions about trimmings, the outfit was ready. I could hardly wait for the first nippy day, so anxious was I to display myself in this gorgeous costume. I imagined the "oohs" and "ahs" I would hear as I stood in front of our building in all my new finery.

A lovely chilly day arrived, and I dressed as quickly as I could in order to take up my post in the street. A glimpse in the mirror, and the little "Narcissus" was ready for her grand entrance. I stood in front of the house and espied my best friend Beverly crossing the street to join me. But what had happened to Beverly? She had always been chubby but now she was rounder than ever. When she reached my side, I realized that Beverly was covered with a fur coat.

As our neighborhood stirred, children and adults alike, passing us would say, "Beverly, what a lovely beaver coat." My eyes began to match my outfit. After a half hour of invisibility along side of Beverlys' glorious raiment, I slipped away and with eyes downcast, returned home to tend my much battered ego.

The second green velvet incident occurred when I was a bride of a few weeks, preparing to move into an apartment near the college I was attending. I was very vague about furnishing my home, but very definite about how the bedroom window was to be treated. The vision of Scarlett O'Hara at the end of the civil war, taking down the green velvet hangings to make herself a presentable gown, was very much in my mind. My mother talked of practicalities such as beds and dressers, pots and pans,

1

For a class assignment, Audrey writes about the meaning of green velvet in her life.

chairs and tables, but I could only contribute one marvelous idea- I had to have lush dark green velvet drapes to close out the world from my new life. I imagine my mother had not read "Gone with the Wind" and she probably didn't realize how versatile the hangings could be.

I did get my way and the green velvet drapes, gathering at my window, were a daily source of romantic imagery.

The third vision of green velvet that comes to mind, is of a housecoat I often wore, which my younger daughter admired greatly. She touched it gently whenever I wore it and dressed up in it often, when I was not at home. I knew this because she could never get it back properly on the hanger. When it was quite worn out, I gave it away and the child often reminisced about its' soft beauty.

Many years later, when she was a college student, I noticed a robe in a shop window, similar to the one she had loved and I bought it for her. She wore it often, but after she married, she left it behind and it still hangs in her childhood closet- a souvenir of the past.

That daughter now has a six year old girl of her own and green velvet covers a span of time and events from my mother, to myself, my daughter and her daughter who bears my mothers' name.

chapter thirteen

Sex

Men want what they can't have.

—*Audrey Volk*

By keeping men off, you keep them.

—*Elsa Schiaparelli*

In August Moon, waiting for our moo goo gai pan, Audrey's on her second Side Car. I take a chance:

"Ma, did you and Dad, you know, before you got married?"

"Are you out of your mind?"

"Well then, did you pet?"

"Really, Patty!"

She explains that a woman must play hard to get:

"If you act like you're interested in a boy, he'll lose interest in you. If you give a boy what he wants, why on earth would he marry you? Once a boy is sure of you, the tables will turn and he'll take you for granted."

Sex before marriage is nonnegotiable. A boy won't marry a girl he thinks is "easy" or "fast." Why should he if he can get what he wants without a ring? Desirability is in inverse ratio to accessibility. A bad reputation follows you all your life. Audrey explains the pathology of gender: "Men only want one thing."

She reinforces the value of a good reputation with the chilling story of Hot Pants:

A freshman at West Virginia University went out on a blind date. She was wearing her new cashmere sweater. The boy was extremely attentive and she'd never felt prettier in her life. He took her to a lovely place for dinner, but on the way back to her sorority house, he pulled off the road. They kissed. When he tried to touch the front of her sweater, she resisted. He kissed her again. This time he put his hand on her back. The next thing she knew, her brassiere had popped open. The following day, word was out. He'd told everybody. By the end of the week she was known all over campus as "Hot Pants." She had to transfer. After college, she got a job in publicity at a venerable publishing house, married a junior editor, and followed him out to California when he got an offer from a major movie studio. There, one evening at a cocktail party, he called her over.

"Renée," he said. "I want you to meet Sid Axelrod. He went to West Virginia too!"

Renée extended her hand. Sid's eyes widened. He turned to Renée's husband and said, "I didn't know you married Hot Pants!"

What this means to me, a ten-year-old's translation, is: It is never okay to have sex before you get married. Never. On the other hand, I came to believe it might be okay to fool around a little bit, to experiment, but not on the first date, and only if you're in love. Given that constraint, when is a healthy girl not in love?

I need to know about sex. Too much is mysterious. Profoundly compelling is my grandmother's Capodimonte lamp. Polly keeps it by the couch in her living room. As family dinners wind down, I disappear from the table with dessert and eat it in privacy by the lamp. The base of the lamp is covered by bulging naked people who are at a party or in a parade or, because they look so sad, on their way to a human sacrifice. Goat-legged satyrs hoist the central figure on their shoulders. This person has a mustache and a full beard as well as a woman's breasts. Is it a man or a woman? Could you be both? If so, could you have children?

Jo leads me into Audrey's bathroom. She opens a drawer and removes a plastic compact. She flips it open.

I'm looking at a beige rubber yarmulke.

"What's that?"

"Mom's diaphragm," she says and tells me what it's for. "When I'm mad at her, I take a pin and stab holes in it. She can't see them but they're there."

"You want her to have more kids?"

"Sure. She hates them."

Most nights, we take baths. But on Saturdays, until my sister turns thirteen, Audrey sets up showers with Cecil. Me, Jo, Dad, the three of us. These showers are exercises in suppressed giggling and trying not be caught staring at Cecil's long purple penis. It dangles there, pointy with a ridge, looking like a map of Manhattan. His scrotum is Queens. I live on my father's penis. West Eighty-third Street is halfway up the shaft. When Audrey is in her seventies, I ask:

"How come you made us take showers with Dad?"

"I was very modest," she says. "I wanted you to be comfortable with the human body but knew I couldn't do it myself."

He calls her "E." She calls him "O." On their matching dressers, they leave notes for each other signed "E" and "O." They refuse to tell us what "E" and "O" stand for. They laugh when we ask, and trade smiles. Are "E" and "O" the noises they make when they make love?

Mom: E! E! E!

Dad: O! O! O!

Are they shorthand for "Oh my God!" and "Eureka!"?

Does "O" stand for "Orgasm" and "E" for "Ecstasy"?

In their eighties, they still won't tell.

They die without telling.

After her husband runs off with Isadora Duncan, Schiap takes a lover, a young married opera singer named Mario. Captivated by an English dandy, she opens a boutique at 36 Upper Grosvenor Street to please him. She sails on a yacht to Scandinavia with "my beau Peter." Back in Paris, she is on the verge of marrying the Spanish consul. "In a frolicking mood," Schiap rents a yacht and invites four men to spend the summer sailing with her. On the *Rayatea,* she does something uncharacteristic: "I let myself go completely." When I read this I think it means she didn't set her hair. Still, I am convinced she enjoys the company of men in a way Audrey would not approve of. I wonder if, since she'd been married and divorced, different rules apply. I sense I'm going to have to make my own way. There is a photo of Schiap sitting on the floor of her living room, next to one of her porcelain leopards. She is looking into the eyes of Adrian Désiré Étienne, the painter and illustrator known as Drian. A look passes between them I know from the movies. I am convinced that look means only one thing.

Sometimes Schiap fails me. In my teens, I can't always count on her. When a boy drives me to a remote spot, turns off the engine and says, "Put out or get out," am I supposed to stumble through dark woods to find my way home? When I dance with a boy who holds me so close I can't breathe, am I supposed to not act on that? Sex is always there, rumbling—like indigestion that turns out to be a heart attack. The little things that say: Not my type. The bigger things that warn you: Stay away. And then the boys with roses in their cheeks, busted noses, hair that curls into a "C" in that smooth spot behind their ears. Boys in engineer boots and torso T-shirts or white Lacostes a size too tight. Boys with inverted spines and, above the waistband of their swim trunks, dimples scooped out on either side, like bookends for the base of the spine. Boys clean or fragrant, boys with hairless backs and ears furled like dried apricots. Their rolling topography and sublime urgent otherness. How willing boys were to make you happy! Boys with long straight toes, boys and their astonishing gravity-defying difference that never loses its power, magic made possible by you. What they want from you is bad for you. But it's what you want too. Sometimes Schiap is no help at all.

We live here. . . .

Design by John Tauranac

Schiap in hostess pajamas, gold wedgies and her favorite emerald necklace, at home with the painter Drian. She commissioned the folding screen from Bébé Bérard.

You look beautiful
sleeping.

I love you

7/28/86

E

Morning note "E" left "O." "O" dated it for his files.

The compelling Capodimonte lamp.

chapter fourteen

Choosing a Husband

She knew she would not marry again. Her marriage had struck her like a blow on the head wiping out any desire to make a second attempt.

—*Elsa Schiaparelli*

I took one look at your father and he was a goner.

—*Audrey Volk*

Dick Adelman is a neighborhood boy, a senior at Columbia Prep. Audrey is fourteen when she falls in love with him. There's a three-year difference in age, but Polly couldn't care less. Audrey is a mature fourteen and the Adelmans are a fine family. Mr. Adelman is a "professional man," a lawyer. And wasn't Polly a married lady by seventeen? Dick Adelman is smart, good-looking and "carries himself well." He's the kind of young man mothers call "husband material." Herman Morgen confers his version of high praise: "The Adelman boy has a good handshake."

Saturday evenings, Audrey and Dick go to parties or the movies or Dick picks up tickets for a Broadway show. Then Polly and Herman grant Audrey permission to take Dick to one of the restaurants for dessert. They double-date with Dick's parents at the Stork Club. He escorts Audrey to his senior prom. During the summer, the Adelmans drive the young couple to their cabana on Long Beach. And then it's September and Dick leaves for Harvard. They promise to write. Sure enough, the first week Audrey gets a short, newsy letter signed "Love, Dick." She waits two days, then writes back and signs hers "Fondly, Audrey." And then there are no letters. Nothing. An agonizing month crawls by. Finally in late October, Audrey spots his blue envelope in the mail. Dick explains that he has fallen in love, it's the real thing, with a Radcliffe girl. "I hope we'll still be pals, Audrey," he writes. "I think you're swell."

Her heart is broken. She'd imagined herself as Audrey Morgen Adelman. She'd sketched pictures of her wedding dress and pieced together what their children would look like—Dick's blue eyes, her straight nose—and how she would decorate their apartment. The monogram on her towels would have been perfectly symmetrical, "AMA," gray against daffodil.

The first time my heart breaks, she consoles me: "If you find something repulsive about someone and focus on it," she says, "you can minimize the pain. You can make the person who hurt you intolerable. Try it, darling. It works."

She explains how she got over Dick. "I focused on his back," she says. "I'd seen him in a bathing suit at the beach.

He had severe acne all over his back. I'd put it out of my mind. Now I welcomed it. He had *craters,* darling. They were *horrible.* I concentrated on them. Soon, whenever I thought about Dick, all I could see was his fulminating back." She shivers a bit. "That's what popped into my mind first."

Audrey has a friend upstairs in the building. Harriet Volk has an older brother at West Virginia University. Audrey fixes her brother, Bobby, up with Harriet. When Harriet's brother, Cecil, comes home for Christmas break, Audrey says, "Wouldn't it be fun if we all went out together?"

The four of them drive up the Hudson and dance to Benny Goodman's orchestra at the Glen Island Casino in New Rochelle. By the time Audrey gets home, she's in love.

The next day she calls Harriet and says: "In five minutes tell your brother to look out his window." Audrey rides her bike on the sidewalk under Apartment 4A. "Hey, Audrey!" Cecil calls, leaning out on the sill. "What are you doing tonight?" A year later, when she graduates high school, Audrey follows him to West Virginia. They marry when, at twenty, he graduates.

AUDREY'S ADVICE FOR CATCHING AND KEEPING A MAN

1. Never write anything to a boy you wouldn't want published on the front page of *The New York Times.*
2. Don't be loud.
3. Never trust anyone, male or female, who says "Trust me."
4. Never let a man see waste in your kitchen sink drain.

5. Always leave some food on your plate.
6. Never tell a girlfriend when you like a certain boy.
7. Never call a boy.
8. Never open a car door yourself or offer to split the check. If you expect to be treated like a lady, you will be.
9. Never do anything with a boy you'd be embarrassed to have him tell his friends.
10. Never criticize a gift, even if you loathe it.

The center of Audrey's life is not her children. And it's hardly her work in the restaurant. Cecil is the axis she spins on, Cecil and the position in the world being married to him affords. Being married to Cecil Sussman Volk is the bottomless blank check that enables Audrey to leave women who married less handsome, less manly, less good-on-the-dance-floor, less successful, less smart, less funny, less courtly and devoted men flailing in her wake. Cecil, the care and feeding of him, the loving and ongoing perfecting of him and the earnest burnishing of their lives together, the hallowedness of their union, is her lifework. Were I to believe my mother, the chance for a decent future hinged on marriage, which hinged on how I looked. The sad truth was, I looked like my father. He was handsome but he was a man. I had broken my nose and was a "mouth breather." As if that weren't bad enough, I went from being "blessed with naturally curly hair" to "frizz-ball" overnight. Lip exercises prescribed by the dentist were imposed to improve "lip rhythm." Something was wrong with my lips. I had no idea what. But ten times a day, I had to tuck them in and hold them tight for ten seconds ten times. My posture stank. I forgot to suck my stomach in. There was no end to what was wrong with me. Like Schiap's family, the older sister was the beauty. In fact that was Audrey's nickname for Jo: "Beauty." It was incumbent on me to develop other attributes.

Young Elsa rarely smiles but boys are drawn to her. She's clever and opinionated. Girls in turn-of-the-century Rome are expected to be demure. She isn't. To the dismay of her parents, she exhibits an independent streak.

On a trip to Hammamet with her father, she refuses the courtship of a Tunisian mogul. She ignores the mooning attention of a Russian prince. She falls madly in love with a young painter who introduces her to the pleasures of port. Celestino does a bit of investigating. He discovers his daughter's seducer is engaged to someone else.

She's devastated but not for long. "I was soon in love again. My youth, my ardor, and a tremendous need of affection made my heart beat passionately for a very young, laughing boy, a real child of the South. Intelligent and warm, he used to come specially for the day from Naples to see me."

But her parents don't like Pino either. Whatever they have in mind for their daughter, it is not a *povero di Napoli*. She is forbidden to see Pino again.

What to do with this willful, impulsive, unattractive girl, twenty-two and on the verge of being an old maid? A friend of Maria-Luisa's has a job for her in England. She will help run an orphanage in Kent and learn English while she's at it. In 1914, Elsa crosses the English Channel. She is immediately charmed by English tea, English courtesy, English trains and, even though she doesn't understand a word, Gilbert and Sullivan. She travels to London every chance she gets. She visits all the museums, and one foggy evening, on a whim, she buys a ticket to a lecture given by Count Wilhelm de Wendt de Kerlor. He is going to speak about theosophy and "the powers of the soul over the body." Elsa is spellbound. At the end of the lecture, the hall empties. She remains in her seat. She can't move. By sunrise, they're engaged.

For the third time, her parents do not approve. She marries de Kerlor anyway. Five unhappy years later, the count and countess sail for New York. Elsa experiences a burst of contact with the new: verticality, steel and glass, the Brooklyn Bridge, the Flatiron Building and neon. She falls in love with the plenty of Woolworth's and the optical magic of barbershop poles. American women are free. They swim, they smoke, they work. In Italy, only the children of the very wealthy are educated, but here the daughter of a poor immigrant can go to school and become somebody.

De Kerlor wanders the streets. No one in America seems interested in his brand of theosophy. He is "a drifting cloud in the sky" until he finds what he is looking for. Isadora Duncan, in front of Elsa, takes off all her clothes and dances for them. Reading this, I try to imagine: Where were they? Where did this private performance take place? A hotel room? Backstage? I can't picture it—a married couple sitting side by side, watching a woman strip?

"From now on," Schiap wrote in *Shocking Life,* "her life would become a series of friendships, sometimes tender, sometimes detached, witty and sharp and short . . . but no man could ever get hold of her completely. . . . She never found the man she needed."

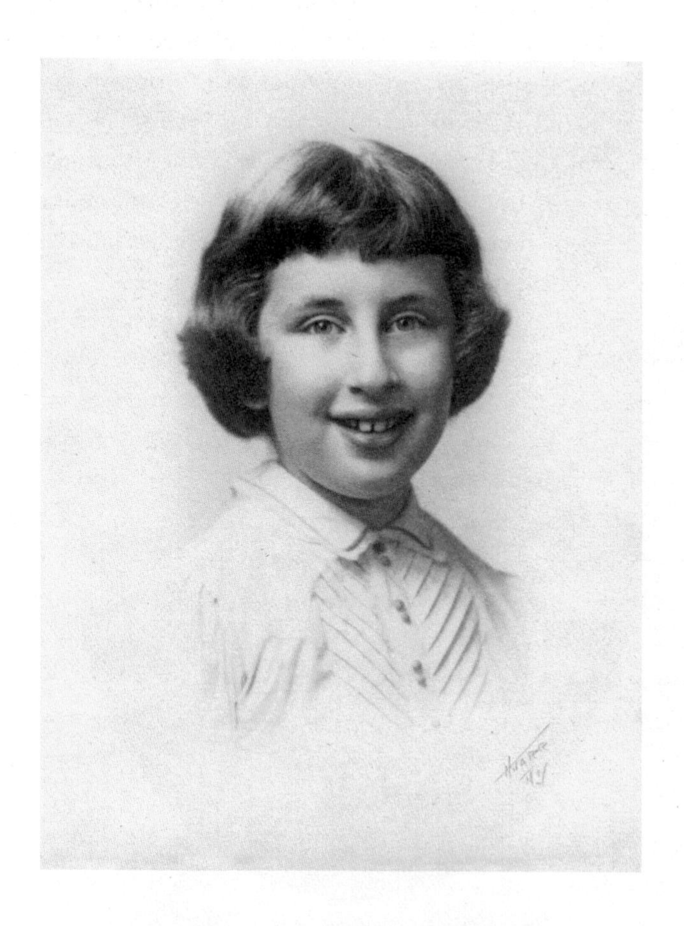

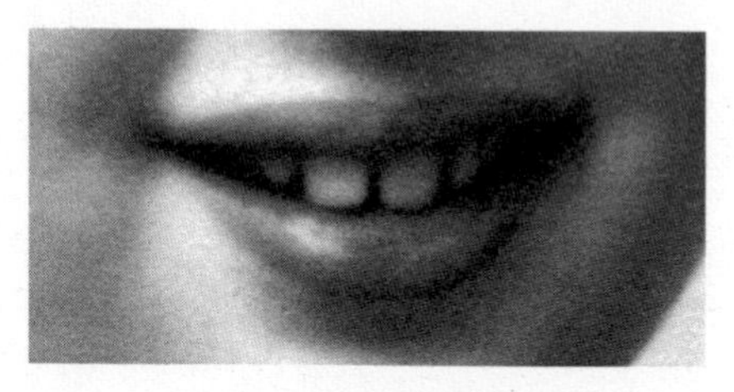

My lips lacked rhythm.

Count Wilhelm de Wendt de Kerlor,
the year he married Elsa Schiaparelli.

Cecil Volk the day he married Audrey Morgen (*left to right:* Speed Vogel, Sid Marcus, Hilly Dubrow, Dad, Joe Vogel, Robert Morgen).

chapter fifteen

Being a Mother

There are two conflicting theories about bringing up children. You can send them to a good school, and keep them there . . . or you can do just the opposite, let them feel the pulse of the world. . . . I believe in the second theory.

—*Elsa Schiaparelli*

Because I said so.

—*Audrey Volk*

There's not a shred of doubt in Audrey's mind: Siblings get along better if they don't compete. She observes her girls then assigns them different areas of expertise. This technique, according to trusted authorities, minimizes sibling rivalry. Audrey cobbles her child-rearing guidelines from Dr. Haim Ginott, Dr. Arnold Gesell, Dr. Benjamin Spock and B. F. Skinner. Thanks to *The Child from Birth to Ten, Infant and Child in the Culture Today, The Common Sense Book of Baby and Child Care* and *The Behavior of Organisms,* my sister is The Pianist, I am The Artist. My sister is The Dancer, I am The Singer. My sister is The Athlete, I am The Reader.

Since my sister is The Dancer, Cecil asks her to dance first. She whirls with abandon like a doll strapped to his feet. Then it's the nondancer's turn:

"Straighten your back!"

"Don't look down!"

"Wait for my signals!"

"That was my *foot,* Patricia Gay!"

"Follow!"

Follow? All those mysterious cues, your right palm cupped in his left, his right hand in the small of your back, subtle incomprehensible pressures on those places, the divining of intent—which cue takes precedence?—the humiliating breakdown of communication and failure of intuition. Follow?

Despite Audrey's research, my sister and I fight daily when we come home from school for lunch. Primarily we use spit, fingernails and shoes. Audrey's punishments descend swiftly or not at all. I begin to understand that if a crime is committed and she doesn't notice or looks the other way, there will be no future retribution. I'm in the clear, that's the end of it. There is comfort in this. I trust it. And there is comfort in knowing that punishments are predictable:

CRIME: Using bad language, saying "lousy" or "Shut up!"

PUNISHMENT: Escorted to the bathroom. Mouth washed with Ivory.

CRIME: Using a tone of voice that makes Audrey say, "I don't like your tone of voice."

PUNISHMENT: A grievous, twisty pinch. (Also deployed for staring.)

CRIME: Backtalk, aka sass.

PUNISHMENT: A hairbrush spanking over Audrey's knees, and once a smack in the face so hard it led to a root canal.

It has not escaped my notice that when my sister is punished she begs for forgiveness. I observe that when that happens Audrey ups the ante. So I roll along and it's beyond okay. Example: Exile for various infractions doesn't feel like a punishment because there are things to do in my room, things most happily done alone: Spy out the window at the lady across the way, tend my tropical fish, write in my diary, draw. I can lick the Tootsie Roll I hide in my shoe bag. This is a scientific experiment. If I lick it once a day, can I make it last a year? I can lie in bed and stare at the world map on the wall and squeeze the continents together until Newfoundland noses into the Bay of Biscay and Lisbon slips into Washington, D.C., and the Kamchatka Peninsula shoves the Shumagin Islands against the Yukon and soon the world is a perfect waterless ball bobbing in blue. There are things to check and things to do. Room jail? Fine! I'll read!

Impulse control doesn't run in our family. Like Schiap, Audrey blows her stack. Suppressing rage? That doesn't occur to anyone. It would require skills uncultivated and not particularly valued. Anger is treated with awe and respect. You better back off. Rage is power. You don't see it coming. It makes me think of snow. You're playing outside and a bit of something small drifts down. One speck. A piece of leaf? Ash? Dust? What could it be? Then you're in a white whirl.

It's hard to trust a mother who has a temper. When she threatens to send me to an orphanage for some infraction, I go to my room and dutifully pack my overnight case. I sit on my bed and wait in my coat. If my mother doesn't want me, I don't want her. After a while I hang up my coat and unpack my bag.

The polio epidemic terrifies New York. It is particularly contagious during the summer. You can get it from swimming in a pool. In the Adirondacks, you swim in a lake. Audrey sends me to sleep-away camp when I am five. Until this moment, I have not taken care of myself in any way. Mattie cuts my meat and brushes my teeth. She dresses me in the morning and bathes me at night. Camp is one mystery after another. In my cubby there is a comb and a see-through tube of Prell, green shampoo with a lazy silver bubble. I stare at these objects and decide the empty spaces in the comb are supposed to be filled with the Prell. I decide Prell is what keeps hair down. Every morning I fill each slot, run the comb through my hair and head for breakfast.

A ritual starts that first summer. I am allowed to go to Levy Bros. on Broadway between Eighty-third and Eighty-fourth Street and pick out a camp toy. From that first summer on, I pick the same one, a doctor kit. Doctor kits come in black plastic doctor bags with twin handles. Sometimes they come in tin valises with hospital cartoons on the sides, but I don't like those. Regardless of the kit exterior, the inside is fitted with a stethoscope, a microscope, tongue depressors, Band-Aids, a plastic hypodermic needle and a bottle of sugar pills. Disposable cardboard cutouts hold them in place. The summer I turn seven, the good kit comes with bad pills—little white beads. The bad kit has good pills that look like real pills in different colors. My favorite thing to do at camp is hold clinic during free time. Girls line up hoping for a candy pill and I get to examine them and make my diagnosis. I have tremendous power giving out those pills to pill hopefuls. Standing in Levy Bros., I switch the pills. I take the good pills out of the bad kit and put them in the good kit. Then I shove the bad pills from the good kit into the bad kit. Once I have the pills I want, I snap both kits closed and join my mother at the cash register.

Did she see me switch the pills? Did she open the kit later and notice the pill bottle didn't fit properly in the cardboard cutout? That evening she tells me that the Levy Bros. detective saw me switch the pills. That Levy Bros. would be sending the police up to camp to arrest me. They had my fingerprints on the other bottle. All the police had to do was match them to my real fingerprints when they got to camp. An open-and-shut case.

And yet: In the second grade, I'm called to the assistant principal's office. Every day for two weeks, Mr. Bloch subjects me to Rorschachs, word associations, mazes, a half-hour of tests a day. The Bureau of Child Guidance has asked Miss Mauk, principal of P.S. 9, for the names of children, one from each grade, who seem particularly well adjusted. My mother and I are chosen to participate in a series of personality tests designed to compare the response patterns of well-adjusted children to those of their mothers.

Parents can't be friends. It's not a level playing field. But at some point, with any luck, you enjoy their company in an easy way. Nobody needs the upper hand. I have this with Cecil, working alongside him in his studio, welding and soldering, making repairs. Drawing and painting. On his motorcycle, we pursue a favorite activity—the quest for clams—steamers, stuffed, fried, chowderized, chewy cherrystones or pearly littlenecks, Clams Casino, Clams Oreganata, Clams Posillipo, bellies and strips, *spaghetti con vongole*—clams in any form. Once in a while, lying next to Audrey in her king-size bed, staring at her ceiling, holding hands, we have stretches like this too. I can ask her anything and she'll tell me. Always I am courteous. Deference is nonnegotiable. "Tone of voice" ranks uppermost on Audrey's List of Requisite Behavior. And much of Requisite Behavior has to do with her definition of "respect." Which makes it all the more puzzling why Audrey treats her own mother a way she wouldn't in a million years tolerate. This is the central mystery of childhood: Why am I expected to treat my mother with deference, yet it is all right for my mother to reduce her own mother to tears? She rages at Polly. She bullies her. She's outright *mean,* and it kills us. We adore our grandmother. We are Nana's *bubbalabens*, her *zezakeppelehs*, her *laben*-on-the-*keppelehs*. We are her *zezakinders*, the loves of her life. Each time Polly gets one of her four granddaughters alone she says, "*You're* my favorite!" We compare notes and laugh, each granddaughter certain she's the one.

"For God's sake!" Audrey screams. "Call Ethel!" "Why are you bothering me, Mother?" "How dare you call me again!" Her voice is a machete. She makes "Mother" sound like a curse. My sister holds me. We cry. If Mattie is around, she studies her shoes, pretending she doesn't hear. When it's really bad, she folds us into her apron. "Don't you know I'm busy?" Audrey shouts into the phone. "I don't have time for this garbage. Call Ida!" And the worst: "What? You're calling me *again*? Is that you *again*, Mother?"(SLAM.)

She spits the words. Her voice curdles steel. Our beloved grandmother can do no right. Nana returns from her first trip to Europe with a breathtaking present for Audrey. She has cradled it in her lap from Paris through Switzerland to Venice, Florence and Rome. She has protected it on planes, trains and gondolas. Audrey glares at the frosted crystal *Vase Bacchantes* from Lalique.

"What do I want a vase with naked ladies on it for, Mother? *Really.*"

She fills it with water for the dog to drink. When the dog gets hit by a car, she puts it under the piano to humidify the case.

I ask my sister the therapist why she thinks our mother was so cruel to hers:

"Mom was a bitch," Jo says. "She used her ability to hurt people to empower herself instead of using her intelligence. Nana was weak. She was cruel to Nana because she *could* be."

The last of that generation, Aunt Barbara, lives in Arizona now.

"Why was Mom so cruel to Nana?" I ask.

Aunt Barbara doesn't respond. She's weighing fidelity to her dead sister-in-law against her niece's need to understand.

"Didn't you notice, Aunt Barbara? Mom always seemed to be angry at Nana. Why was that?"

Aunt Barbara dips a toe in: "Your mother wanted everything to be perfect," she says. "Hair. Clothes. Nana didn't care about perfect. Nana was earthy."

"She was? *Nana?*"

Nana, with her chic suits and lavish furs and big diamonds, was "earthy"?

"Your mother could be very strict with Nana if her hair or clothes weren't right." Aunt Barbara picks up steam. "Perfection was a necessity. If Nana wore pink and green together, your mother let her have it."

Does Aunt Barbara believe this? Is this the best she can do?

Audrey volunteers for Class Mother every year. She doesn't miss a single play or trip. And even though she thinks washing her girls' mouths out with soap is the progressive way of setting limits, even though she hits so often my nickname for her is THOON (The Hand Out of Nowhere), I love her and am proud of her. She's on my side. She tests me for the spelling quiz. She protects me from my sister and punishes Jo for pummeling me. I'd rather be with Audrey than just about anyone. The precision of her language excites me. I can make her laugh. She loves my hair.

And yet, and yet: When we're shopping together and Audrey runs into an acquaintance, if she doesn't like the way I look that day, she pretends she doesn't know me. She turns her back. She doesn't introduce me. I'm not there. I peel off and paw the racks. My mother pretends she is shopping alone.

Once, lying in bed, looking at her ceiling, I ask her if she has any regrets.

She thinks. Finally, she says, "One."

I'm hoping she regrets the way she spoke to her mother or that she apologizes for the time she THOONed me in the mouth for sassiness. The aftermath of that whack, the resulting root canal, led to an ongoing prosthodontic challenge.

"What is it, Ma? What do you regret?"

"That I talked my mother out of getting a face-lift."

When Gogo is six, she says, "Mummy, where is my father?"

By then Count Wilhelm de Wendt de Kerlor is dead.

Schiap tries to explain the notion of death to a six-year-old. When she is finished, Gogo looks up at her and says: "Well, after all, you are my father and my mother."

Gogo attends school in Switzerland. Occasionally Schiap will visit and treat Gogo and her friends to a good meal. Schiap creates the "Go-Go Doll" and dresses her in tiny versions of Schiaparelli couture. A predecessor of Barbie, Go-Go is an eight-inch vinyl walker with sleeper eyes and rooted hair. She comes with outfits and accessories for travel, ballet, all kinds of activities. Everything the Go-Go Doll wears has a tiny Schiaparelli label sewn inside, including her real-fur cape.

When Gogo is ready to meet men, Schiap sends her beautiful gowns. A London newspaper, the *Daily Express,* asks Schiap to write an open letter to Gogo on the correct way for a young lady to dress:

> *Dear Gogo,*
> *Soon you will be buying your own clothes, so, considering the time I spend worrying about clothes for women—some of whom I never even see—I suppose I ought to give you a little advice.*
>
> *To begin with, you won't have a big dress allowance because I think it is a bad thing for young people (maybe for all women, I'm not sure). It takes them longer to acquire judgment if their mistakes*

cost them nothing. Up till now you have been wearing tailor-mades most of the time. Well, that is not a bad habit for anyone. Don't allow yourself to react from it too violently. Your first inclination will surely be to buy as much as you can for your money. Don't give in to it. . . .

You can only get to know good clothes from bad by looking at good ones. So, when you see a smart woman, study her. Only the rich can afford cheap clothes. If something you see looks worth twice its price, you may be sure the illusion will not last. What you buy must be good. Cut is of the first importance, and cut of course implies fit. Suits, coats, dresses, cut by an expert, fitting you perfectly, will stay smart long after the fashion which they follow is forgotten.

I will not give you a list of colors which "will go" and those which will not because I believe that any one color will look well with any other provided (and this is, I think, the secret) that both are good clear, clean colors.

Five years old, at sleep-away camp with a head-full of Prell. You were safe from polio in the Adirondacks.

224 East 28th Street
New York 16, N. Y.
July 11th, 1950

Mrs. Cecil Volk
110 Riverside Drive
New York, N. Y.

Dear Mrs. Volk,

In connection with a research project on which I am currently engaged Miss Mauk, Principal of P.S. 9, gave me permission to give personality tests to a number of children in her school who seemed especially well adjusted. Patty was one of those selected.

In as much as we are interested in knowing more about the mothers of well adjusted youngsters it is important at this point for us to compare the response patterns of the children with those of their parents. Would it be possible therefore for you to come to the office of the Bureau of Child Guidance at 224 East 28th Street on Tuesday afternoon, July 18th at two o'clock to help us by taking the same personality test? The crosstown buses transfer to the Second Avenue bus which stops at our corner. We are also near the 28th Street station of the Lexington Avenue subway. Our telephone number is Murray Hill 3-4791.

You may be assured that the results will be held confidential and used only for research purposes. Of course no names will be revealed.

I would appreciate it greatly if you would be willing to co-operate on this project which we hope will contribute to a better understanding of parent-child relationships.

Sincerely yours,

Kathleen Lolis

(Miss)Kathleen Lolis

Letter to Audrey from the Bureau of Child Guidance.

The *Vase Bacchantes* by Lalique.

Audrey in Claire McCardell. Her mother in fox-trimmed cashmere. Does she look earthy to you?

My favorite photo of my mother
and me, and a painting of it.

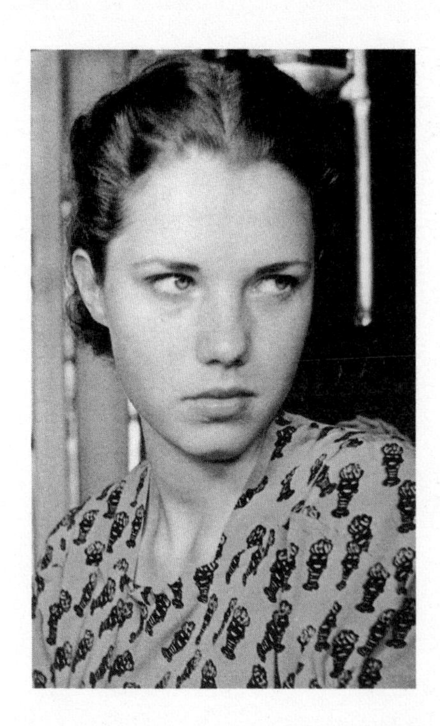

Gogo Schiaparelli and her namesake doll, an eight-inch walker with rooted hair and sleeper eyes. Schiaparelli labels were sewn into all of Go-Go's costumes, including her pink rabbit-fur stole.

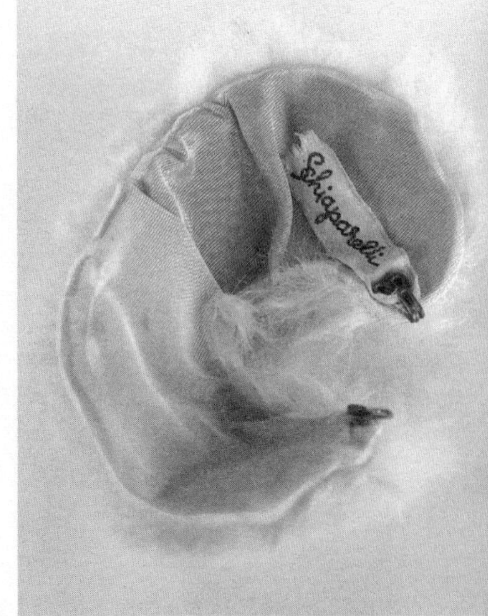

chapter sixteen

Superstition

Never put a hat on a bed.

—*Audrey Volk*

Truly mystic, she believes in IT, but has not yet found out what IT is.

—*Elsa Schiaparelli*

Audrey is agnostic. Sometimes she refers to herself as *an* agnostic. "I'm not sure there is a God," she says. "Frankly, darling, I doubt His presence." We celebrate Christmas. Our tree pulses with bubble lights and tinsel. What Audrey believes in, the closest she comes to organized religion, is superstition:

"If you leave the apartment, then remember you've forgotten something, when you come back in to get it, you have to go into the bedroom and, just for a moment, sit on the bed."

"If you're walking down the street holding hands and

something comes between you—say, a lamppost or somebody walking a dog—when you reclasp hands, you have to say 'bread and butter.' "

"The open side of a pillowcase must always face away from the door."

"Step over the legs of a growing child? Why not just lie down in front of a speeding train?"

"A red ribbon tied on a baby's crib keeps the evil eye away."

"It is all right to brag about the baby, provided you spit through your fingers three times. You needn't actually expectorate. You can symbolically spit by saying 'Toy! Toy! Toy!' through the 'V' of your first two fingers."

Schiap's superstitious too. She designs a line called Lucky Dresses, printed with the Big Dipper. Four is her lucky number: "I saw it, loved it, and felt I belonged to it," she said, buying her eighteen-room mansion at 22, rue de Berri. "The number in the street was my lucky number: 22, two plus two equals four."

Ready to announce a new perfume, Schiap is certain "the name had to begin with an 'S,' this being one of my superstitions." A color for the packaging is needed too. Schiap imagines a pink that is "bright, impossible, impudent . . . like all the light and the birds and the fish in the world put together, a color of China and Peru but not of the West—a shocking color, pure and undiluted." She gives artists work whenever she can and sets René Clément to the task of making the new color. He develops four interpretations—cameo pink, desert rose, ruby pink and mauve. Schiap turns all of them down. She says no to the next three too. She wants a color that's never been seen. How do you make a new color? How do you describe it? Is there a vocabulary? Once you've seen an oil slick or a Madagascar panther chameleon, you suspect the color wheel is covered. Try to picture, say, a dark yellow. And yet Professor Mas Subramanian at Oregon State University recently made a new pigment. As reported in the *Journal of the American Chemical Society,* manganese oxide mixed with other chemicals and heated to two thousand degrees Fahrenheit produces a brilliant new blue.

Schiap is convinced it can be done. She sees the new color in her head. It must electrify. Clément nails it on the eighth try, a mixture of a particular magenta with a particular pink. There are countless magentas and pinks. Clement mixes the magical ones in the magical proportions. And there it is, the color Schiap dreamed of. She knows it when she sees it, the brightest, clearest deep blue-pink in the world. It becomes her lucky color. Her next collection—every gown, every shoe, every handbag—is this color. Schiap owns it. Decades later, acknowledging its power, Yves Saint Laurent will say, "She alone could have given to a pink the nerve of a red."

Using her lucky "S," Schiap calls the color "Shocking Pink." Every Schiaparelli scent begins with her lucky letter: Si, Soleil, Sleeping, So Sweet, Succès Fou, Salut, Scamp, Sans Souci, Santé, Spanking, Snuff (the first perfume for men, presented in a glass pipe in a cigar box) and Sport After Shave. Zut! (which in English loosely translates to "Holy Toledo!"), starts with the "S" sound.

For luck, Schiap never travels without an empty cold-cream jar. It protects a crumpled picture of Joan of Arc given to her by a man she met in Hollywood.

Peacock feathers augur "disappointment and bad luck."

She does not allow lilacs at 22, rue de Berri. If someone sends her lilacs, the servants are instructed to donate them to a hospital and bring Schiap the card. But one afternoon she comes home and discovers a vase of lilacs in her living room. The next day, two poplar trees in her courtyard mysteriously crash down and the Germans march into Paris.

My mother doesn't own any Schiaparelli hats, dresses or jewelry. She's no fan of Schiaparelli lipsticks, perfume nips (small glass pipettes for single applications) or beauty creams either. She doesn't go for the perfumed charms, or rings you slip Shocking-scented cotton into so the scent wafts when you move your hand.

What Audrey does have is what Schiap envisions for the woman who can't or won't pay five thousand dollars for a House of Schiaparelli gown: Something lovely and amusing from Elsa Schiaparelli. And what Audrey does have, I think of as lucky: In addition to her "Shocking" perfume and cologne, she has Shocking sachets, lingerie envelopes and compressed bath sponges (drop one in the tub and it blooms like a flower, scenting the whole bathroom, expanding until suddenly you've got yourself a full-size pink washcloth!). She has Shocking Pink heart-shaped guest soaps packed in pleated white paper cups like bon-bons, and Shocking dusting powder. The motif on the powder box is four hearts almost kissing at their pointed ends, repeated over and over, like wallpaper, four hearts, a family of four, like Audrey, Cecil, Jo and me, our family, the four of us. Piercing each heart where you'd expect to see an arrow is a gold sewing needle. A fine blue thread pokes through the eye. It loops around each heart spelling out "les parfums Schiaparelli paris france" in thread. The letters fall the way a thin thread would if you actually looped letters out of it. Fifty-two hearts (I know. I count them) about to kiss. There are fifty-two weeks in a year. You have to look closely. Everything Elsa Schiaparelli designs has more meaning than first meets the eye. Everything Audrey has from Schiap is worth studying. The more you look, the more you see.

Before she leaves our apartment, Audrey scents her handkerchief with a drop of "Shocking" cologne. She unscrews the top, places her hankie over the hole. With a flick of her wrist she inverts the bottle. Her hankie, for good luck, is perfumed for the day.

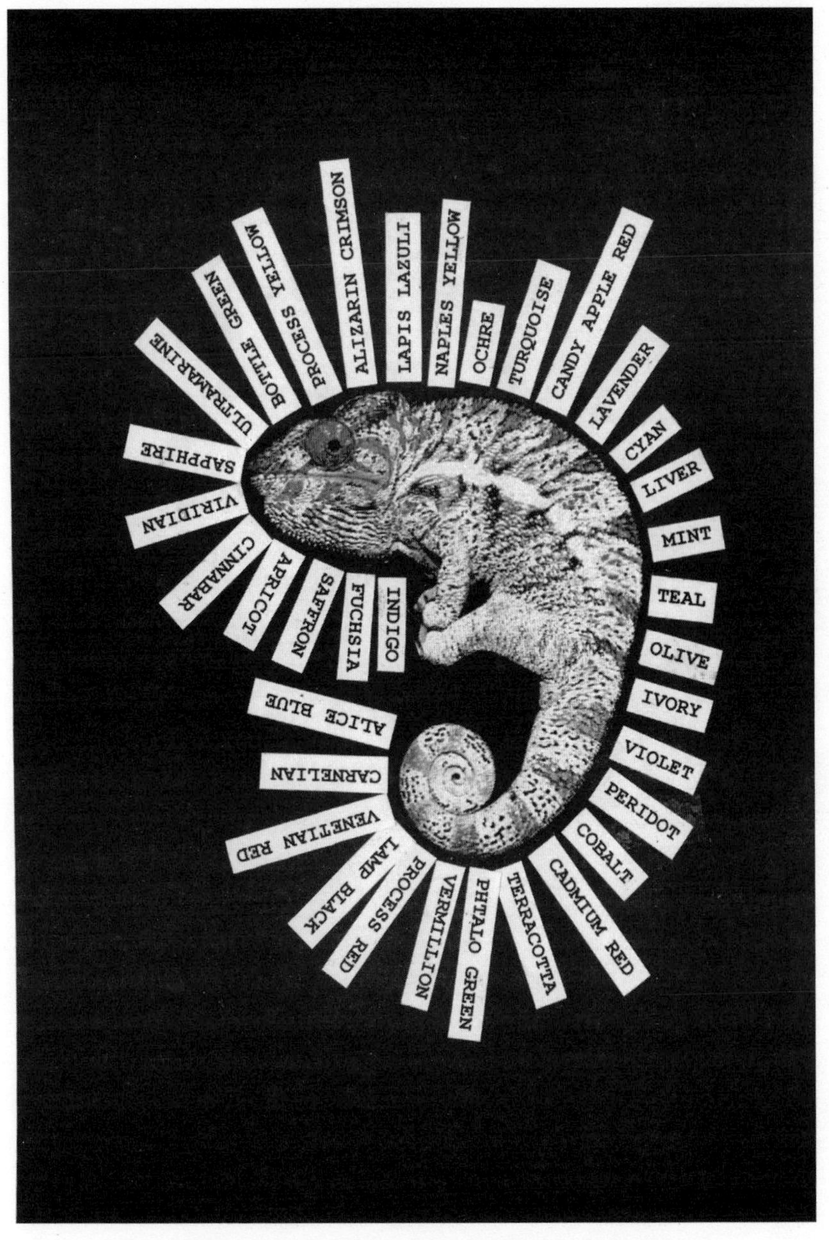

The Madagascar panther chameleon (*Furcifer pardalis*).

chapter seventeen

The Bogomoletz

One never knows what the effect of a Bogomoletz will be. Sometimes it makes the hair grow black, sometimes it turns hair white, sometimes it makes one feel younger, but at other times it makes one swell like a whale.

—*Elsa Schiaparelli*

Are you making yourself useful?

—*Audrey Volk*

On January 17, 1944, *Time* magazine reports a discovery: The director of Kiev's Institute for Experimental Biology and Pathology has invented a miracle drug. He is decorated with the Order of Lenin and the Hammer and Sickle Gold Medal. Anti-reticular cytotoxic serum (ACS) is made from the bone marrow of human corpses. It speeds healing, increases all the body's defenses and may enable man to live to 125.

Schiap reads about Professor Alexander Alexandrovitch Bogomoletz in New York during the war. The United States Embassy has persuaded her she is at high risk in Paris. In 1941, Elsa Schiaparelli, Italian by birth, French by choice, outspoken critic of fascism, flees. She keeps the doors at 21, place Vendôme open. She wants to save as many jobs as she can. Undercover, Schiap wends her way to Lisbon, then flies into Idlewild Airport aboard the Dixie Clipper.

But what will Schiap do in New York? She reads about Bogomoletz: "One must not lose desires," he says. "They are mighty stimulants to creativeness, to love, and to long life." Schiap needs desires. She needs something to be passionate about. Her Bogomoletz takes the form of submerging herself in charitable works. In New York she designs uniforms for the Salvation Army. She gives blood. She judges a sewing contest at the Waldorf-Astoria. On the CBS radio show *Report to the Nation,* she begs Americans, in a teary voice, to send needles and thread to France. She embarks on a cross-country lecture tour, to raise money for French children. She joins a relief organization called American Aid to France. In the Whitlaw Reid Mansion at 451 Madison Avenue, she stages art shows and concerts that demonstrate links between French and American culture. She asks Marcel Duchamp to install a Surrealist art exhibit. Her budget is small. Duchamp gets a good price on sixteen miles of cord. With the help of his friends André Breton, Max Ernst and Alexander Calder, they string it back and forth, up and down, weaving a web from chandeliers and columns and easels and back. The viewer is ensnared in front of the pictures like a fly in a web, a surreal experience looking at Surrealism.

Schiap experiences her major Bogomoletz by enrolling in

a program at the American Red Cross. "I learned how to take a temperature, how to treat a burn, how to bandage a broken leg, how to stop a wound flowing, how to revive a drowned body. . . ." She tests blood and bathes the dying. One of her biggest challenges is something I do without thinking at camp, making the perfect hospital corner. Hospital corners baffle Schiap: "a geometrical problem not easily solved." Mornings at six, Elsa Schiaparelli walks to Bellevue Hospital in white sneakers and a nurse's uniform for a full day of "endless stories, swamped in organic smells—all this made her feel part of humanity again, and no longer a dead branch hurled by the hurricane, and it saved her soul." You can't be miserable when you're doing good. Schiap is rejuvenated. She feels useful. She writes: "This particular Bogomoletz gave Schiap courage and to a certain extent made the difficult years tolerable."

Audrey could use a wartime Bogomoletz too. Her twenty-four-year-old brother, Bobby, is shipped to Saipan. Herman Morgen closes his restaurants, all three of them, refusing to deal in black-market meat while his boy is overseas. Polly bans flowers in her home. Cecil opens the Robert Cecil Bakery with the understanding that half the profits are to be put into a savings account for Bobby when he comes home. No one in the family will buy anything made in Germany. Herman Morgen switches from Heineken to Miller High Life—"The Champagne of Bottled Beer." Yorkville and its *Konditorei* are off-limits. Going crosstown for Schwarzwälder piflinger is out of the question. The ban includes Chanel N° 5. Although Chanel N° 5 is made in France and she is French, our family despises Coco Chanel. She is a traitor. Firing her staff, closing her *maison,* it is common knowledge that she is riding out the Occupation in the arms of the Nazi spy Baron Hans Günther von Dincklage, aka Spatz. From their love nest at the Ritz, using von Dincklage's influence, she does her best to steal the House of Chanel from her backers, our *landsmen,* the Wertheimers, who own 70 percent of everything Chanel. While the rest of Paris starves, Chanel nibbles *fraises des bois.*

"Can you imagine?" Polly says, pouring her Chanel N° 5 down the drain. "That *momzer.*"

Nana switches to Bellodgia, a floral yet spicy scent made by the House of Caron.

When the war is over, Chanel is accused of being a traitor, *une tondue, une collaborateur horizontale.* She is arrested by the Comité d'Épuration. After questioning, they release her. If the Comité decides she is guilty, she will be arrested again, her head will be shaved and she will be paraded through the streets of Paris in her underwear. While the Comité is deciding how to proceed, Chanel receives a phone call warning her to leave Paris immediately. She and von Dincklage speed by car to Switzerland. It's an ongoing mystery—to this day no one knows for sure—who made that call and how Chanel and von Dincklage were allowed to cross the border. According to Hal Vaughan in his book *Sleeping with the Enemy: Coco Chanel's Secret War,* it was Chanel's good friend Winston Churchill who saved her: "One theory has it that Chanel knew Churchill had violated his own Trading with the Enemy Act (enacted in 1939, which made it a criminal offense to conduct business with an enemy during wartime) by secretly paying the Germans to protect the Duke of Windsor's property in Paris."

In 1954, after nine years in exile, Chanel returns to Paris. She is greeted with less than love. French reviews of her first collection say she has "lost her touch." The British call her line "mumsy." Courrèges likens her to "an old Rolls, still in working order, but inert." Lillian Ross interviews Chanel for *The New Yorker* and asks her why she stayed in retirement so long: "Her brown eyes flashed. 'Never was I really in retirement in my heart. Always I observed the new clothes. . . . Always I was smiling inside my head, and I thought, I will show them.' " It's the Americans who embrace Chanel's immaculately tailored, modernistic suits. Americans save the House of Chanel. They don't seem to care about Chanel's politics. When I ask Rosamond Bernier about this, she says: "At the end of World War II, no Americans knew what was going on."

Despite the wartime gloom and the anxiety about the well-being of her brother, Audrey has one secret smoldering joy: Cecil is safe. Six family stories circulate. Dad does not serve in World War II because:

1. He has high blood pressure.
2. He is an alcoholic.
3. He isn't an alcoholic but shows up at the draft board blotto and swears he is.
4. Audrey goes to the draft board, throws herself on the

floor, writhes and cries: "You can't take him! He has two babies! I'll kill myself!"

5. Audrey goes to the draft board, throws herself on the floor, writhes and cries: "You can't take him! He's an alcoholic with high blood pressure! If you take him, he'll be more trouble than he's worth!"
6. When he was ten, Dad had an orchiectomy after being kicked by a horse. The army doesn't want a man missing a testicle.

Cecil could drink. Appearing at his draft board slurring his words and tripping over his feet would have been a walk in the park. But even after Pearl Harbor and the wave of patriotism that followed, there must have been plenty of men who didn't lust to sign up. Wouldn't coming in drunk be the first thing a draft board would suspect? As for Audrey's writhing on the floor, it's not easy to imagine. A histrionic display would have been out of character. And yet were stakes ever higher? Audrey would go to any lengths to protect Cecil. She adored him. I suspect she could not have imagined life without him. What would she be, a young widow with two baby girls and no source of income? She would be the worst of the worst, the lowest of the low, the phrase she used for women worthy of abject pity. She would be *damaged goods.*

Cecil never had high blood pressure. He maintained 100 over 70 till he died. Is it possible to give yourself, with the right medicine, a temporary case, high blood pressure for a day? Dr. Freddie King, who treated four generations of our family, who relished weekends with my grandparents at the Shelburne in Atlantic City and the Al-Bur-Norm on Schroon Lake, was an ethical man. But might he have been willing to help Cecil, especially since our family already had one son overseas? Amphetamines make your heart go crazy. Every dieter knows that. What is it like for Dad, a strapping twenty-three-year-old, to sit out the war in New York? How does he respond when people say, "Why aren't you overseas?" Does he start with "I tried to enlist, but . . ."? And what does Audrey say when people ask, "Where is your husband stationed?" followed by "Why isn't he serving?"

Most often, she tells story number four. And like Schiap, she thrusts herself into good works. Being purposeful is the antidote for shame. Good works are Audrey's Bogomoletz too. She knits socks. She becomes an officer in the Bread Donor Nursery and Junior League for Child Care. She runs the Bookmobile at Polyclinic Hospital and makes sure her girls have a job too. We are to collect all the thin metal strings smokers pull to open the cellophane on a pack of cigarettes, every single one we can find. We walk looking down. We scour our block. We pester the elevator men. The Riverside Drive playground at Eighty-third Street is a gold mine. Jo and I are human metal detectors prowling the benches where mothers sit and smoke. We find them, triumphant, silver or gold and sometimes red (Lucky Strikes). We are told these metal strings will be melted down into bullets. I want mine to make the bullet that kills Hitler.

When I ask Dr. Michael Cohen, my internist, what pill a man could have taken in the 1940s that would have temporarily raised his blood pressure high enough so he would not be draft-worthy, he says: "You wouldn't need a pill. If you don't drink any water for a day and then run four miles, you dehydrate yourself and your blood pressure will rise." The last time I overhear Audrey tell a Why Cecil Wasn't Drafted story, she uses version number one. We thought it was a miracle that, after four and a half years in a trench, Uncle Bobby came home. He was never right again, but gladiolas reappeared in my grandmother's living room and Herman Morgen opened a big new restaurant in the garment center where, since Schiap's New York office was around the corner, most likely she had lunch.

Postwar, my grandmother sticks with Bellodgia. Nothing German enters our homes until, eleven years after V-E Day, Cecil rolls into the driveway on a BMW motorcycle. No one mentions it is made in Germany. My father wants the safest bike. If he is going to engage in the dangerous act of motorcycling, it behooves a responsible family man to ride the sturdiest bike there is. My son drives a BMW station wagon. My daughter brews her coffee in a Braun. I've lost my taste for Pflaumenkuchen. But when my friend Benjamin Taylor's mother dies, he disposes of her beautiful things in one generous afternoon, appointing them to his ladyfriends, and I come into possession of Annette Bockstein Taylor's quilted Chanel shoulder bag.

In 1971, Chanel dies in her suite at the Ritz. She is seventy-seven. She dies with a caved-in face, features squashed together like the puppet Señor Wences made out of his hand. She dies with the face she deserves, a mean little greedy face made absurd by plucky straw boaters and giant earrings emblazoned with two gold "C"s, which, to my mother, grandmother and me, stood for "Coco Collaborateur."

The "First Papers of Surrealism" show, in 1942, at the Whitlaw Reid Mansion in New York. Schiap put Duchamp on a tight budget. He bought sixteen miles of string and used one. Then he hired twelve children in sports gear to play ball, jump rope and chase each other. If asked what they were doing there, Duchamp told the children to say, "Mr. Duchamp told us we could play here."

Selective Service

Local Board No. 34
88 West End Avenue
New York, N. Y.

YORK, N.Y. SEP 7 6:30 PM 1944

(LOCAL BOARD DATE STAMP WITH CODE)

OFFICIAL BUSINESS

Cecil S.

REGISTRATION CERTIFICATE

This is to certify that in accordance with the Selective Service Proclamation of the President of the United States

Cecil Sussman Volk
(First name) (Middle name) (Last name)

845 West End Av New York NY
(No. and street or R. F. D. No.; city or town, county and State)

has been duly registered this 16 day of Octo 19...

J B Valle
(Signature of registrar)

Registrar for 24 11 New York N
(Precinct) (Ward) (City or county) (State)

BE ALERT { Keep in touch with your Local Board. Notify Local Board immediately of change of address.

CARRY THIS CARD WITH YOU AT ALL TIMES

D. S. S. Form 2 16—17105

Dad's draft notice.

DESCRIPTION OF REGISTRANT

RACE		HEIGHT (Approx.)		WEIGHT (Approx.)		COMPLEXION
		6 1/2		190		
White	✓	EYES		HAIR		Sallow
						Light
Negro		Blue	✓	Blonde		Ruddy
		Gray		Red		Dark
Oriental		Hazel		Brown	✓	Freckled
		Brown		Black		Light brown
Indian		Black		Gray		Dark brown
				Bald		Black
Filipino						

Other obvious physical characteristics that will aid in identification

NOTICE OF CLASSIFICATION

Cecil Sussman Volk
(First name) (Middle name) (Last name)

Order No. 11718 has been classified in Class 2A

(Until 19)
(Insert date for Class II-A and II-B only)

by ☐ Local Board.
☒ Board of Appeal (by vote of ___ to ___)
☐ President.

Sept. 7, 1944 S. L. Kushen
(Date of mailing) (Member of local board)

The law requires you, subject to heavy penalty for violation, to have this notice, in addition to your Registration Certificate (Form 2), in your personal possession at all times—to exhibit it upon request to authorized officials—to surrender it, upon entering the armed forces, to your commanding officer.

DSS Form 57. (Rev. 3-29-43)

Cut along this line to detach card

Description of registrant and classification.

In his novelty act, the ventriloquist Señor Wences made a dummy out of his hand. It bore a startling resemblance to Coco Chanel.

chapter eighteen

Reckoning

Had I not by pure chance become a maker
of dresses, what could I have become?

—*Elsa Schiaparelli*

I never expected my hands to look like
this. Whose hands are these?

—*Audrey Volk*

As soon as she can get a flight, Schiap books passage back to France. The war is over. She heads straight for 22, rue de Berri to see what's left. She has no idea what she'll find. Have her trompe-l'oeil tapestry walls been painted white? Did the Germans smash her mirrors for spite? For three years, they commandeered her home.

Alone, she walks through every room. Miraculously, everything is intact. Downstairs, in the front hall, she pauses.

The drawer of her console is filled with calling cards left by French friends who visited during the Occupation. Schiap cuts every card-leaver dead.

At the place Vendôme, she doubles all salaries and launches her Talleyrand Silhouette. Jean-Paul Sartre asks her to design costumes for his new play, *Le Diable et le bon Dieu*. *Vogue* calls Schiap "the only true artist in fashion." To celebrate the liberation of Paris, she collaborates with Dalí on her most dramatic perfume presentation: Press the catch. A gold scallop shell yawns to reveal a Baccarat bottle. The dauber is the sun. Its bursting rays are hand-gilded. The features of the sun's face are composed of Schiap's symbol of freedom, birds in flight. The base of the bottle is the rippling ocean. Waves crest in blue enamel. "Though too expensive and too sophisticated for the general public," she wrote, "it was a lovely object destined not to die."

Schiap calls this presentation "Le Roy Soleil." Two thousand Sun Kings are produced and sell out immediately.

She sends a bottle to one of her best customers. A thank-you note is hand-delivered:

> *Dear Madame Schiaparelli,*
> *It is really the most beautiful bottle ever made, and the Roy Soleil is a very lasting and sweet gentleman. I cannot tell you how much I appreciate your giving me such a handsome present which has displaced the Duke's photograph on the coiffeuse! I shall be back again either tomorrow or Friday morning.*
>
> *With every good wish for great success*

with your collection which deserves all the applause.

I am,

Believe me,

Yours sincerely,

Wallis Windsor

At Paramount Studios, there's talk about making a movie of Schiap's life. It will star Joan Crawford, who continues to wear Schiap's tray shoulders long after Schiap tells her, "You must give them up, Joan. They are *vraiment passé.*" Later, another Schiap client, Lauren Bacall, is proposed for the lead but the movie is not made. A young cutter named Pierre Cardin, said to be excellent with scissors, joins the House of Schiaparelli. A promising twenty-year-old named Hubert de Givenchy is hired as a junior designer. "Surrealism was finished by then," said Givenchy. "When I arrived at the house and saw her wearing two different color shoes, I said to myself, 'How can a woman with so much talent not understand that that is all over?' " Schiap, creator of the themed collection, brings out six a year: the Broken Egg Silhouette, the Gibson Girl Look, the Mummy Silhouette, the Riding-Habit Line, the Hurricane Line, the Arrow Silhouette. Twenty years after she's on the cover of *Time,* she's on the cover of *Newsweek.* A survey in front of the New York Public Library confirms that "Schiaparelli" is the best-known name in fashion. But something is wrong. Something has changed. The clothes aren't selling. Schiap misjudges the postwar woman. Theatricality and what Schiap christens "hard chic" are no longer calling cards in a freshly chastened world. Impudence and conspicuous luxury have lost their glow. Insouciant clothes misfire. Schiap is out of touch with the prevailing mood. "I tried to make women both slim and elegant, so that they could face the new way of life. I did not immediately realize that the sort of elegance we had known before the war was now dead."

Still she can't quit. Incapable of compromising on quality, ignoring her advisers, she pushes Schiaparelli, Inc., deep into debt. Schiaparelli perfumes begin supporting the House of Schiaparelli. In 1947, a young designer named Christian Dior announces his "New Look." Youthful, straightforward yet feminine, it hits the right note. Schiap hears "the tolling of the bell." The House of Schiaparelli becomes moribund. For the first time, suppliers refuse to extend credit. Bankruptcy looms. In 1954, with much prodding from her trusted business manager Monsieur Cavaillé-Coll, the House of Schiaparelli closes its doors at 21, place Vendôme.

It's devastating to see her fail. Even when I am little, I know that if life is going to be any good you've got to love your work. And here Schiap is, doing what she loves, answering to herself and failing.

Why couldn't she change with the times? I don't get it. I look at my grandmothers and wonder why people get locked into ideas. Granny Ethel still wears her hair the way she did when she was seventeen. Nana Polly still loads her handbag every morning as if war is about to be declared on Manhattan.

There will be no more House of Schiaparelli couture.

There will, however, be more Schiaparelli than ever. Schiap reinvents herself. She becomes a licensing pioneer. Elsa Schiaparelli leases her name to Playtex girdles, Cutex nail polish, Glentex scarves, Kimberly-Clark, Formfit, Wyler's Foods, Nomotta Yarns, Congress playing cards, Arrco playing cards, Sealy mattresses, Longines watches, paper dolls and real dolls, Catalina swimsuits, Doeskin gloves, fabrics, furs, stationery, shower curtains, cars, eyeglasses, table linens, lingerie, Vat 69 Scotch, Good Luck margarine, Kraft Italian dressing, Westcott Hosiery Mills, menswear, ties, cuff links, handbags, hats, jewelry, shoes and chewing gum.

Cecil agonizes over it but eventually decides the time is right. He's going to sell the restaurant. He's spent two killing years negotiating a twenty-year lease, and now he can retire with an income. He sublets Morgen's West. Overnight it becomes an Italian restaurant that sends him a big fat check every month. No more getting up at 5 a.m. to haggle with his suppliers then print the day's menu. "PPP," Cecil likes to say: "Prior Planning Pays."

Audrey has done her preparation too. Armed with her M.S.W. and the prospect of a new career, she puts their house on the market. Two professionals come in and stage a marathon three-day tag sale.

"Mom, you're selling the Morganti Brighton Banjo Barometer?"

"It hasn't worked in thirty years."

"The Syrie Maugham sofa?"

"What do I want with a Syrie Maugham sofa in Florida?"

"Not Granny Ethel's bronze pheasant!"

"When you need a bronze pheasant, you can buy your own."

They fall in love with a McMansion in Boca Raton. It has soaring ceilings and white marble floors. The tiles measure two feet by two feet. They're set on the diagonal like diamonds. The lines make me dizzy—there are no right angles in this house. It's crazy-making where the tiles meet the walls, which are designed not to be plumb. The house feels off-kilter, but not to them, and God!, how they love it, all forty-eight hundred square white feet of it. Moby Home. Four bedrooms and five bathrooms, a restaurant-size kitchen, breakfast room, TV room, two offices, a huge dining room and living room—all surfaced in a color born to show dirt. Even though she has a housekeeper, Audrey bends a thousand times a day, picking up a crumb or a hair or a bug on its back no one else can see. She's like one of those perpetual-motion bird toys that peck water out of a glass. Up-down, up-down, she folds at the waist. "It's good exercise," she says, marching a sesame seed to the sink.

They have twelve of their happiest years before Cecil gets paged at his club. He is to report to his doctor's office immediately. It's not good. A routine blood test has come back with seriously elevated numbers. Cecil has acute myelogenous leukemia. Overnight he goes from playing three sets of tennis a day to chemo "cocktails." He loses his hair and his strength and parts of his skin. Each time something doesn't work, Dad tries something else. Jo and I are typed for bone-marrow transplants. He's accepted into an experimental protocol.

When my great-grandparents die, one right after the other, I'm little and can't figure it out. Where did people go?

"How can they just disappear?" I asked my mother.

"They don't," she said. "They're in you. Every generation that precedes you. Sometimes in ways you don't even know. It could be anything, darling. A turn of phrase. Not liking nutmeg. People don't disappear. Look how you hold your pinky."

I looked down. "It's just like Poppy!"

"Exactly."

Cecil weathers treatment after treatment until his doctor comes up empty-handed. The day Dad dies, Audrey dictates a message for my sister to record on the answering machine. Audrey regards Jo's speaking voice as the best. "A finely tuned instrument," she calls it.

"Cecil succumbed to leukemia at five-thirty this morning," my sister says into the phone. "We are unable to return your call."

I fly down to Boca once a month now. More when my mother breaks a bone. She is valiant going it alone. But she no longer has the strength to walk around her enclave with me. A year ago, she was leaving me in the dust. She begins to laugh when she mishears something, turning it into a little comedy or drama:

"You said 'sticker'? I thought you said 'liquor.' Ha-ha!"

"You said 'tennis courts'? Oh my God! I thought you said 'cold sores.' "

Either she's getting shorter or I'm getting taller.

There is one thing I want. Something I want her to give me.

"May I have this?" I ask.

Cue number one: Her lips tighten.

It is impossible to pick up the check when we go out for a meal. Shopping with her, if she approves of your selection, Audrey whips out her AmEx card. A driver picks me up at the airport in West Palm and he's prepaid. My mother is wildly generous in unpredictable ways but doesn't appreciate being asked for something. Not one bit. No, she most certainly does not, uh-uh.

I wag the bottle at her.

She raises an eyebrow—cue number two.

Now I'm supposed to put the bottle down and say, "Oh, it's not important." Or "I don't really want it, Ma. *N'importe, chérie.*"

I'm good at reading her. Better than my sister. It's possible reading my mother is what I do best. I know what might displease her and sense it the way trained dogs can predict an epileptic seizure. I know what makes her laugh. I am tuned like a Stradivarius to her flickery moods, innuendos, all shifts therein. I bat a thousand predicting her responses. She can't surprise me, not anymore. I am the curator of her cues, the cue connoisseur. I know them all.

Whatever I just said about Audrey and me is counterbalanced by my sister. Two accidents born eighteen months apart, sharing a bedroom, going to school, tap class, and camp together, we might have been born to different people. My sister thinks strict obedience is the shortcut to love. For me, that price is too steep. Pleasing our mother is like trying to eat Jell-O with chopsticks. My sister courts Audrey. She lays her slim, beautiful neck on the block. Mom's ax catches the sun. Doesn't Jo know? In an autobiographical sketch for one of her writing classes, Mom wrote: "My anger is easily ignited. In fact, I enjoy the preliminary sensations—the prickling scalp, the blood rushing to my head, and the tremors in my limbs that foretell the beginnings of a fine rage."

Aha, I tell Jo, reading this. *Rage is Audrey's sex.*

Aha, Jo tells me, reading it. *Audrey is a sadist.*

Doesn't she get that anger thrills our mother? My generous sister offers herself, a human sacrifice. She is enraged by our mother yet covets her approval. She wants to be what Audrey wants her to be, regardless of price. My sister is guaranteed to come back for more. But Audrey knows she can alienate me. I am capable of being more remote than Cassiopeia. "You left town early on," Jo Ann recently told me. "You went into outer space. You saw what was happening to me and you didn't like it. You were a pearl spinning nacre."

So I smile at my mother and raise my eyebrows back at her. Whenever I smile, I wonder if she notices the tooth. It's the lower-right central incisor. My mother never says anything about that tooth, even though she criticizes the other ones. "Boy," she laughs when I smile, "you've sure got a lot of gold. Get me my sunglasses." But the tooth that is beginning to look strange, the root canal from fifty years ago, is an eyesore. Mom's mum. This tooth Audrey never says a word about.

It's confusing when someone you love hits you so hard you need a root canal. It's confusing when someone you love hits you so hard you need a root canal and doesn't apologize. It's confusing when someone you love hits you so hard you need a root canal, she doesn't apologize and says, "If you're ever rude to me again, I'll knock the other thirty-one out." Especially because you know that person loves you. The person who wouldn't think twice about insisting you take her seat in a lifeboat can also kill your tooth. It would mean the world to me if she apologized. A dam would break. "She never will," my sister says. "Give up."

I hold the bottle. Usually I ask for nothing. Audrey knows this. She hasn't used this bottle since 1955. I love this bottle. I suspect she's aware of that. Sometimes she gives me things she knows only I will cherish: the wool cap my father bought her at Le Château Frontenac on their honeymoon, Granny Ethel's surreal silver salver that looks like a celery leaf, her wedding dress with a waist so small it was too tight to button on my wiry eight-year-old one Halloween. I'm the one. My mother chose me for these things. Jo doesn't care about them. Audrey knows that. Just because my sister is vulnerable doesn't mean she's sentimental.

I stand there holding the bottle. I don't say a word.

Mom's look says, *You should know better.* She is on her continent of a bed, a California king covered by a custom silk quilt. It resembles the quilts Mr. Oswald, her New York quilt man, used to make. Three generations of our family used him for their beds. Everyone agreed he was an excellent quilt man. Mr. Oswald made house calls. Now in Boca Raton Mom has found a quilt lady. Mrs. Gutierrez comes to the house with swatches and she sews silk quilts too.

Reading in bed is still sacrosanct. The shaded sconce makes Audrey's cap of hair look gold. She stares at me over her readers. Propped by pillows, she is in one of her many pristine white Oscar de la Renta peignoir ensembles. All of them are the same, her beauty-sleep uniform. She is spending more and more time in bed. She sleeps with oxygen tubes in her nose, and now she keeps them on during the day too, but only in her bedroom, only in front of her daughters and her aides. She won't go shopping with the tubes or play bridge in them. My brilliant sister invents cushions out of pink foam hair rollers to cover the tubes where they press into Mom's face. That way, when company comes or she goes out, Mom won't have red lines from the tubes denting her cheeks. The doctor has told her that using the oxygen round the clock will take some strain off her weary, compromised heart, but my mother has rules for how she will appear in public. And my mother has told me—as she has lost the ability to play tennis, to walk around her enclave, to shop at Bloomingdale's, as her illnesses have progressed and multiplied (she has lymphoma, hemolysis, pulmonary hypertension, neuropathy, osteoporosis, congestive heart failure, and arthritis in two fingers—making them curl), as she has begun to breathe like a fish on a dock, as she has qualified for a disabled parking spot, as filling the thirty-five compartments of her weekly pill organizer has become an activity and her new way to measure the passage of time—my mother has told me, "I'm quite happy to live as long as I can still do three things: play bridge, do *The New York Times* crossword puzzle and read." These three things are enough. If she has nothing left but her trifecta, she can be content. She loves bridge. She is a member of the American Contract Bridge League and the World Bridge Federation. She goes to local tournaments with her girlfriends and wins enough Silver Masterpoints to become a Sectional Master. She'd like to be a Life Master, but that would mean earning three hundred or more Masterpoints, of which at least fifty must be Silver (she has those), at least twenty-five must be Gold, and at least another twenty-five must be Red or Gold. For Red and Gold points, she has to go to regionals. This entails traveling and staying overnight in a hotel. She's willing but there's a problem: Audrey simply will not share a hotel room with any of her bridge partners.

"They don't want to pay full-price for a room," she explains.

"So treat your partner to a room, Ma."

"It would change the dynamic."

"Tell them it would be your pleasure."

"They would feel beholden."

Audrey, as superb a bridge player as she is, will never scale the Life Master heights.

So we look at each other. It's what she calls "a Russian standoff." I'm determined not to break the silence. I could seesaw the bottle like it was dancing and say, "Please, pretty please with sugar on top?," and make her laugh, but I don't want to. I use the absence of speech with my mother the way Native Americans used it, to make the other person hear what they've said, to maintain dignity.

She shakes her head as if I'm hopeless. "What do you want it for?"

"I love it."

"What are you going to do with it?"

"Nothing."

"Fine." She waves me away with the back of her hand and returns to her book.

There's less than an inch of perfume left, but the bottle of Elsa Schiaparelli's "Shocking" cologne is mine.

I take it into the guest room. I unscrew the top.

I raise the bottle to my nose and take a whiff. Quickly I

put the top back on. The smell of "Shocking" has not changed. It is still there in this bottle, a genie, heavy and rich, floral and spicy, the smell of my mother. That night I call my sister: "Mom gave me her bottle of 'Shocking.' "

"What did you want *that* for?"

"I'll be able to smell her whenever I want."

"But she hasn't worn 'Shocking' in years. She stopped wearing that when they came out with 'Norell.' She stopped wearing 'Norell' when they came out with 'Paris.' "

"How do you remember that?"

"Please," she says. "I'm a therapist. I have to remember the names of my patients' *dogs*."

"But 'Shocking' is the smell of our youth," I explain.

My sister disagrees. She says when we were little our mother's smell was Pall Malls. "And when she read in bed in the afternoon, the air from between her legs."

I kiss my mother goodbye. At the airport, Security asks me to step aside. A man rifles my carry-on. His hand stops.

"What's this?"

"My mother's perfume. What's left of it. She gave it to me."

He unscrews the top and sniffs. "You're not supposed to carry more than three ounces of liquid on the plane."

"Oh, this is much less than that. It's less than an ounce."

He hesitates.

"See?" I say. "It's almost empty. When it was full, then it had four ounces. But now, it's less than a quarter filled."

I could lose this bottle. It could get tossed on the mountain of gels, lotions and cuticle scissors, the Great Airport Confiscation Heap, the amnesty loot bag. What do they do with all that stuff? Airport Security must be the best-groomed service group in the world. My mother's "Shocking" is slipping through my fingers.

"Look." I dig out my travel shampoo. "This is a bottle I bought at Target especially made for flying. See?" I point to the airplane on the label. " 'Airline Security Approved.' This one always goes through, and there's more shampoo in this little bottle than perfume in this big one."

I hold them side by side.

"I don't know . . . ," he says.

" 'Three-ounce travel bottle,' " I read the Target label. " '*Bouteille de voyage de* eighty-nine milliliters. *Botella de viaje de* three ounces.' "

I point to the contents in the "Shocking" bottle. "One ounce," I say. "Maybe even half. Half an ounce, tops."

"That's a much bigger bottle." He points to the "Shocking."

"Yes! It is! You're right! But it's almost empty!"

"I'd call that a six-ounce bottle," he says.

"Okay," I say. "I can go to the ladies' room and rinse out the shampoo from the three-ounce bottle and put the perfume in it, and then the big bottle will be empty. Would that be okay? An empty bottle? Want me to do that? I can do that. I'm happy to do that. Will you let me back in line at the front?"

He puts the "Shocking" in my bag and zips it up. "Next time your mother gives you perfume," he says, "put it in a smaller bottle."

Dior's New Look from 1947.
Waist = 18 inches.
Bust = 36 inches.

Postwar women failed to see the charm of the Broken Egg Silhouette.

APRIL 15, 1938
137
Schiaparelli SPONSORS Cutex Tulip FOR SPRING
"Wear it with your gay prints, with pink, dusty blue, purple, brown and yellow"
With an unerring eye for the chic, the wearable—Schiaparelli, famous Paris dressmaker, sponsors the new Cutex TULIP, to wear with her newest and loveliest Spring clothes. She is famous for a sixth sense that enables her to catch Tomorrow's tempo. So you may be quite sure that Cutex TULIP will be utterly right for the clothes and mood of the coming season!
Vibrant . . . Keyed to Springtime
The fresh, glowing color of full-open red tulips—little cups of bright red in brilliant Spring sunshine—sings in the new Cutex TULIP.
You'll adore this tender, gay TULIP shade with your new bright prints. It will be perfect, too, with this season's high-fashion purples, with dusty blue, with the new Spring pinks, and with both brown and yellow. We have Schiaparelli's emphatic say-so for this.
So—all of you—wear lovely, glowing Cutex TULIP—sponsored by Schiaparelli—and be in tune with the gay new Springtime world.
Cutex TULIP, like all Cutex shades, goes on with delightful smoothness. And stays on—without fading, chipping or peeling. Be sure to see all the chic new Spring, 1938 Cutex shades! Only 35¢ a bottle.
Northam Warren, New York, Montreal, London, Paris
PRINTED CREPE IN PURPLE, BLUE, PINK, CORAL ON DARK BROWN
YELLOW JACKET, BROWN SKIRT—WOODEN "SABOTS" BUTTONS
PINK WOOLEN SPORT SUIT
MAUVE CREPE—PURPLE SILK-JERSEY GLOVES
CUTEX
CUTEX
Try these Six Exciting New Cutex Shades
HEATHER: A deep, smoky rose, with a hint of purple in it, for your navy, beige or gray suits.
LAUREL: Ashes of roses, a subtle smoky pink. Lovely with Spring pastels, gray, beige.
CLOVER: Deep, luscious red—goes beautifully with everything except orange tones.
THISTLE: Rust and Rose have met and mingled. Perfect with gray, green, rust, brown
TULIP: A fresh, glowing red. Stunning with black, pink, blue, purple, yellow, brown.
ROBIN RED: Truered, subdued in intensity. It really goes with everything.
Also Rose, Old Rose, Rust, Natural, Colorless and Burgundy.
Go to your BEAUTY SHOP
What a good dress designer can do for your figure, a professional manicurist can do for your fingers. Any shop displaying this sign will give you an Authorized Cutex Manicure.
CUTEX

Schiap pioneered the celebrity endorsement.

My mother's bottle of "Shocking" cologne.
The Airport Security–approved travel bottle.

chapter nineteen

Through the Looking Glass

I merely know Schiap by hearsay. I have only seen her in a mirror. She is, for me, some kind of fifth dimension.

—Elsa Schiaparelli

I'm not afraid to die. Not at all. I don't expect you to understand that now, but you will.

—Audrey Volk

Here she is at the rest of her life. Schiap travels. She boards a DC-7 toting the Elsa Schiaparelli "Jet Wardrobe": six dresses, one pair of shoes, three hats and a reversible coat for day and night, weighing in at less than seven pounds. She visits friends all over the world and comes to a stop at her seaside retreat in Tunisia, Hammamet, where her father had taken her half a century ago. She examines her life and wonders something impossible to know: What would have happened if she'd been a painter or a sculptor? She thinks she is excellent at both. In the end, she decides she is, after all, an artist: "Dress designing . . . is to me not a profession but an art."

Returning to Paris, Schiap flings open the doors of 22, rue de Berri and welcomes her friends. She settles in to write her memoir. When she is sixty-four, *Shocking Life* is published in England and the United States. The reviews come in. They are what Audrey would call "less than wonderful":

> For those readers who enjoy reading about newsworthy personalities, there are glimpses of many such figures. . . . For the most part, it is the author's own personality which emerges and the reader will enjoy the book if this unpredictable, restless, talented and essentially unhappy woman strikes a sympathetic chord.
>
> —Agnes Rogers, *New York Herald Tribune*

> Accept Madame Schiaparelli's irritating ego and exaggerations. Chalk them up to the Latin flair for drama, and "Shocking Life" provides a turbulent entertainment, a serious glimpse of the workroom side of a French high fashion *atelier.*
>
> —Leo Lerman, *The New York Times*

> It is clear from the places and names mentioned in Mme. Schiaparelli's autobiography, and from her reputation in the world of fashion, that she has had a fasci-

> nating career, but she tells her story so disjointedly that one cannot help wishing she had employed somebody to translate her experiences and her personality onto the printed page.
>
> —*The New Yorker*

> It will not be surprising if Schiap turns out another book—in which case perhaps she'll see to it that the seriousness of its content is matched by its title and appearance.
>
> —Elizabeth Hawes, *The London Times Literary Supplement*

Schiap does not turn out another book.

What designer does a former designer wear? Schiap admires the work of two: Cristóbal Balenciaga and a Moroccan newcomer, Yves Saint Laurent. Both consider it a privilege to dress her. Early on in his career, once he was certain he wanted to be a couturier, Balenciaga bought Schiaparelli dresses to study how they were made. And Yves Saint Laurent credits Schiap with his favorite design, "Le Smoking," a man's smoking jacket cut for women to wear in the evening. Schiap introduced hers in 1936. Thirty years later, Saint Laurent re-created it for Catherine Deneuve.

"Schiaparelli never stopped hitting Paris in the face with the most ideal form of provocation," Saint Laurent wrote in his foreword to Palmer White's biography of Schiap. "She slapped Paris. She smacked it. She tortured it. She bewitched it. And it fell madly in love with her."

Schiap reads. She is content to watch almost anything on television. She visits Gogo and her son-in-law, Robert Berenson, whom she calls "Berri," like her street. And she gets to know her granddaughters. They're growing up. Berinthia (nicknamed Berry but with a "Y") will marry the actor Tony Perkins and become a photographer. Her older sister, Marisa Berenson, becomes a high-fashion model, New York's "It" Girl of the 1970s, and then a movie actress. For a while Marisa shares quarters with Schiap on the rue de Berri. It isn't easy:

"You're going out in *that*?" the woman who designed and wore the see-through dress says to her granddaughter.

In 1972, when she is eighty-two, Schiap has a stroke. She throws herself into rehabilitation and makes a vibrant recovery. But the following year, she's felled by a second stroke. And this time she is unable to do what Audrey would call "martial her resources." Schiap is bed-bound. Friends stream in to visit. She receives them from beneath her covers, meticulously coiffed, in a satin bed jacket. Always there are vases of fresh flowers. "Shocking" fills the air.

And then, in September, Elsa Schiaparelli has a third and final stroke. She falls into a coma. Seven weeks later, on November 13, 1973, she dies in her bed. Gogo is holding her hand. It's said that on their deathbed people cry out for their mothers. Schiap calls for someone else, her friend from long ago, the *povero di Napoli* her father forbade her to see: "Pino! . . . Pino!" she cries. "Is that you?"

The November 13, 1973, front page of *The New York Times* has the following headline:

KISSINGER SAYS U.S. WEIGHS PACT TO DEFEND ISRAEL

Two days later, Schiap's obituary makes the front page too:

SCHIAPARELLI DIES IN PARIS; BROUGHT COLOR TO FASHION

Elsa Schiaparelli is laid to rest in a graveyard in France, behind a small stone church in the village of Frucourt, in the region of Picardie. As always, no detail is left to chance. Schiap visited the site beforehand to check its suitability: type of trees, their age and location, the proximity to a dear friend's home, the look of the headstones, the care of the grounds. The quiet, the ambience. All aspects met with her approval. But there is something else, something meaningful enough for her to choose to be buried in a tiny town two hours north of Paris: The *cimetière* is named after Saint Eloi, the patron saint of collectors of gold coins.

Schiap's final creation is her tombstone. Her bold signature is chiseled then gilded across a gray limestone slab piebald with white fossils from the sea.

Audrey doesn't sound right on the phone. I head for the airport. Jo drives up from Coral Gables. We rendezvous for lunch. I pick up sandwiches from the deli Audrey prefers, the one with the mayonnaisey coleslaw, and we picnic on her bed. She talks to us with her eyes closed. She wants her daughters to be "fiscally responsible" like she is. She tries, one last time, to teach us about money:

"GOs are the best munis because they're fully backed by the state," she says. "The best notes are project notes backed by the government, six months to a year. If you buy on the secondary market, you get paid immediately. Now listen, girls: There is a table of commissions. A broker will give you a discount if you generate a lot of business."

Her eyes flitter open. She takes us in.

"Do you understand, girls?"

"Got it, Ma."

"I don't believe in mutual funds, girls. You're giving people money to keep your money. Am I making myself clear?"

"Uh-huh."

"And remember this, girls. Never give all your money to *one* money manager. Jo Ann? Patty? Are you listening?"

We exchange glances. Her money lessons are intense and from the heart. We do our best to focus. We nod in what we hope are the right places and thank her profusely. We know we're pathetic. Two women who have more than once been the sole supporters of their own families, we know how to make money. That said, we have no idea what she's talking about.

"Things will be easier for you when I'm dead," she says.

Easier for you when I'm dead? Is she dying? Does she mean after she dies we won't have to worry about her? That not worrying about her is preferable to having her? Does she mean life will be easier with no more frenzied trips to the emergency room? No more flying down for every broken bone and Mohs procedure? No more seeing her in pain? Or wait, is she talking about money? We've just been talking about money. Is it money? Financial security? We don't ask. Anything she wants us to know, she tells us. We have no idea what her assets are. What she calls "moneytalk," specific numbers, is crude. Moneytalk is verboten, always has been. Specific financial information is private. Now that our father is dead, no one knows what Audrey has except Audrey and her trusty accountant, Bonnie. We think she puts her money into AAA-rated tax-free municipal bonds and lives on their safe, predictable income. But that's a guess. We've observed her slitting open her brokerage envelopes and smiling. What are "GOs"? What are "project notes"?

Easier for you when I'm dead? What does that mean?

"All right, girls." It sounds like she's giving up. "I've done everything I can for you. I've told you everything I know. I have nothing left to tell you. Are you sure you understand?"

"Yes," we lie. "Absolutely, Ma. We get it."

Then we go into a guest bedroom and close the door. We bend over, holding our guts, and silently laugh our heads off. We gasp for air.

"What the hell was she talking about?" my sister says.

"You're asking *me*?"

She can no longer make it to her bridge games. Her friends offer to drive her, pick her up, to bring lunch, to wheel her, whatever it takes. But Audrey has no zip. Breathing, even with the oxygen, is work. "I'm . . . miasmic," she tells me over the phone. This is as close as she comes to complaining. I look up "miasma" in the dictionary. The second definition is most apt: "a noxious atmosphere or influence *wreathed in a miasma of cigarette smoke*." I imagine my mother stumbling through fog-filled moors. She remains curled in bed in her white satin gown which is where I find her, newly tiny, folded like a fetus, when I fly down.

I kiss her cheek. "I love you, Mom."

"I'm . . . miasmic, darling," she whispers. She doesn't open her eyes—too much energy. My mother reaches out her hand for me to hold.

"Can you do the puzzle?" I ask.

"No."

"Can you read?"

"No."

"Want me to read to you?"

"No."

I get in bed next to her and hold her hand. I kiss it. I stay for three days and make her favorite lunch: BLTs on toasted whole wheat with lots of mayo and salt and burnt bacon. She barely touches them. Eggs won't go down. Even applesauce. Before I fly home, my mother says, "There's something you can do for me, Patty."

She wants me take her car to the luggage store and buy her a suitcase. Specifically, she wants the largest version of my suitcase. I'd been telling her for years to get the kind with wheels and dispose of her saggy needlepoint set. Whenever I pick her up at LaGuardia, I have to wrestle her behemoths to the cab. You can't hoist them off the conveyor belt without saying "Oy." Mine's a roller with a collapsible handle, lightweight, waterproof. I've got the small and the medium but would never spring for the large.

"Where ya going, Ma?" I ask.

"I'm going to get better and come visit you," she says.

"I'd love that."

"I want the large one, darling." She bobs a finger at the handbag on her chaise. "Take my card out of the wallet."

I charge the large one on her AmEx. She never uses it. She never comes to New York again. Later on I understand. She wanted me to get her the large one so I would have the full set when she died. Who will want for me like my mother again? The following year, I use all three pieces on a trip to China. A stranger on the tour says to me, "I can tell you're rich."

"I am? You can? How?"

"Your luggage matches."

Audrey would have called that woman "common." But she would not have minded that her daughter was perceived as rich.

When I'm back in New York, the phone rings: "I told the doctor, 'I don't care . . . if it shortens my life. . . . You have to give me something. . . . This is no . . . quality of life. . . . I have no . . . *energy*.' "

The doctor prescribes Viagra. The next day Mom leaves a breathy message on my phone machine:

"I feel wonderful, sweetheart! I just got back from Bloomingdale's! Doraleen pushed me in the *chair*!"

For the first time in six weeks, she walks into her office. She catches up on paperwork, ebullient. She leaves the office forgetting she must take a step down to enter her sunken living room. She falls and breaks her pelvis on the white marble floor. This is her fourth major broken bone in three years. It goes through the skin.

Jo speeds to the emergency room. She sits by Audrey's side for seven hours.

"Go home," my mother says.

"I'm not going," my sister says.

"I don't want you here. Get out, damnit! Get out *now*! I need you here like a hole in the head! *Go!*"

An hour later, Audrey tells her nurse: "Kill me. Get a baseball bat and hit me in the head. I mean it. I want you to crush my skull."

"I can't, Mrs. Volk," the nurse says. "It's against the law."

"I'm *asking* you to. Don't you *see*? Get a witness. She'll testify I *asked* you."

The following day my mother's beleaguered heart can't take it one beat more.

When she was in her fifties, Polly bought eight plots, six of which currently idle at the Mount Pleasant Cemetery in Westchester. Nana's will stipulates that only family can lie beside her. I suspect she was thinking her children and their spouses would keep her company, along with her widowed sister Gertie and her last living brother, Jerome. She was forward-thinking in many ways, but Polly failed to anticipate the population explosion, recession and cremation craze. My mother has no headstone. She is scattered in the Atlantic at 25°38.552N by 80°11.863W, the precise point we scattered Dad five years earlier, almost to the day.

I decant Mom from the plastic bag and tie her ashes, along with one of her pocket mirrors, into a scarf Raymond Nedjar, an old French boyfriend, gave me. It is one of those tourist scarves that have the Eiffel Tower, Notre Dame and the Arc de Triomphe on it, places I visited on my first trip to Europe with my mother as tour guide, the trip when I met Raymond in Cannes. Mom was a first-rate travel companion. She could walk all day and wanted to see everything. She knew European history. She was ever-game. We had the best time.

I sew four of my favorite buttons—one that looks like a diamond, her grandmother's Gripoix, the grape button from her trousseau, a lavender one from her engagement dress—to the corners of the scarf for weight. I tie the corners together, then wrap the scarf in her wedding headpiece. It's shaped like the top half of a heart, two scallops covered in lace, seed pearls and faux orange blossoms. Mom wore it a bit forward. It tied under her chin with a giant tulle bow, à la Schiaparelli.

I drop the bundle overboard. It does not sink as planned. My mother knocks against the hull. I say goodbye. The captain starts the engine. His girlfriend surprises us by pitching hot-pink rose petals over the side. Mom bobs in a Shocking Pink petal escort. I keep my eye on the flotilla until it sinks or drifts out of sight. I don't know which. It is one or the other. It is not possible to tell.

I'm not going to tell you what year this was, the year Audrey died. Far be it from me. If I told you the year you might be able to figure out her age and Audrey would say, "That's none of your business." There's enough in this book that violates her confidence already. Audrey's age, revealing it, for a woman like my innately private mother, my beloved mother, my outrageously beautiful mother—really, don't you know? That would be the last straw.

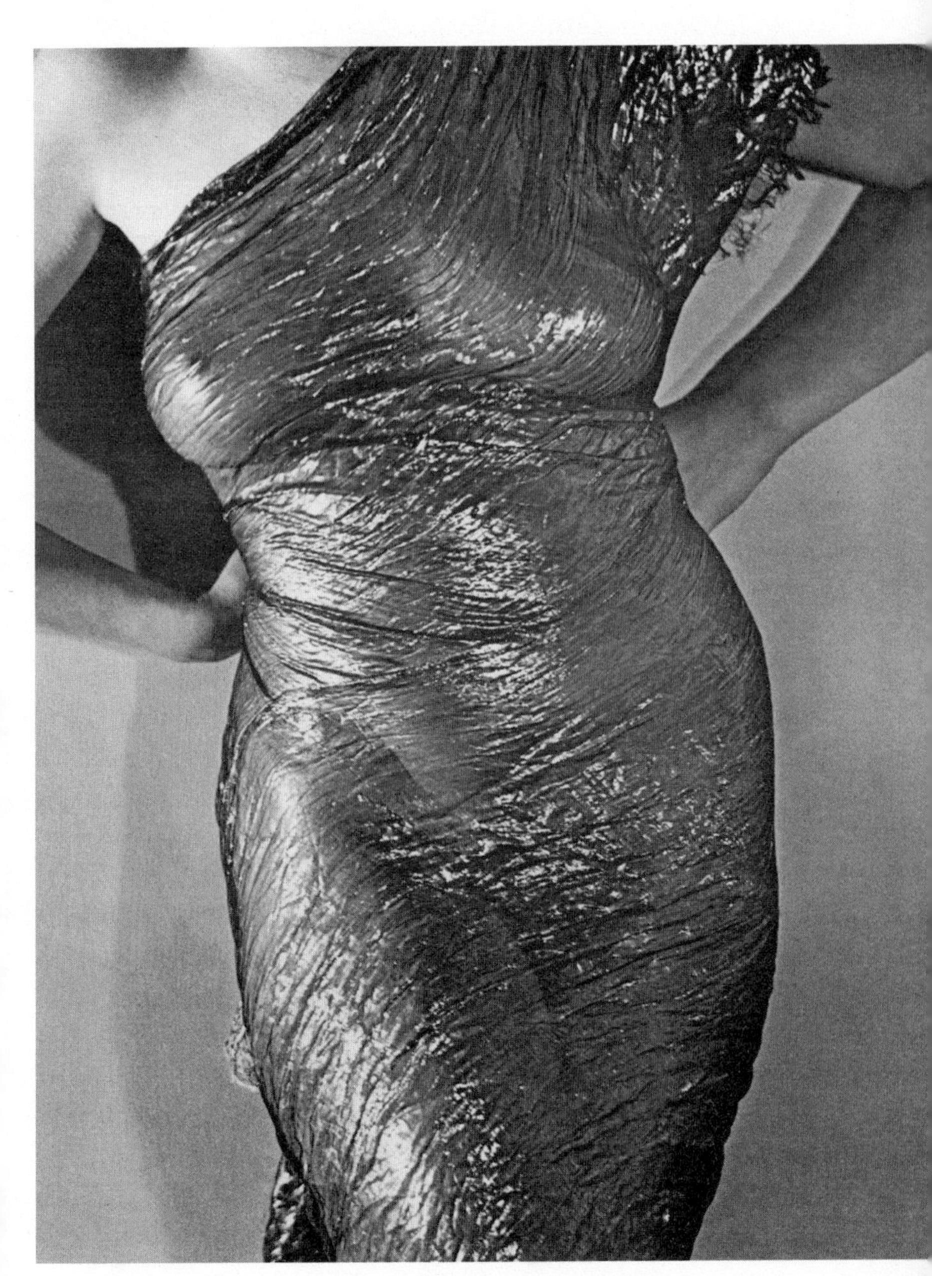

Schiap in her cellophane dress.

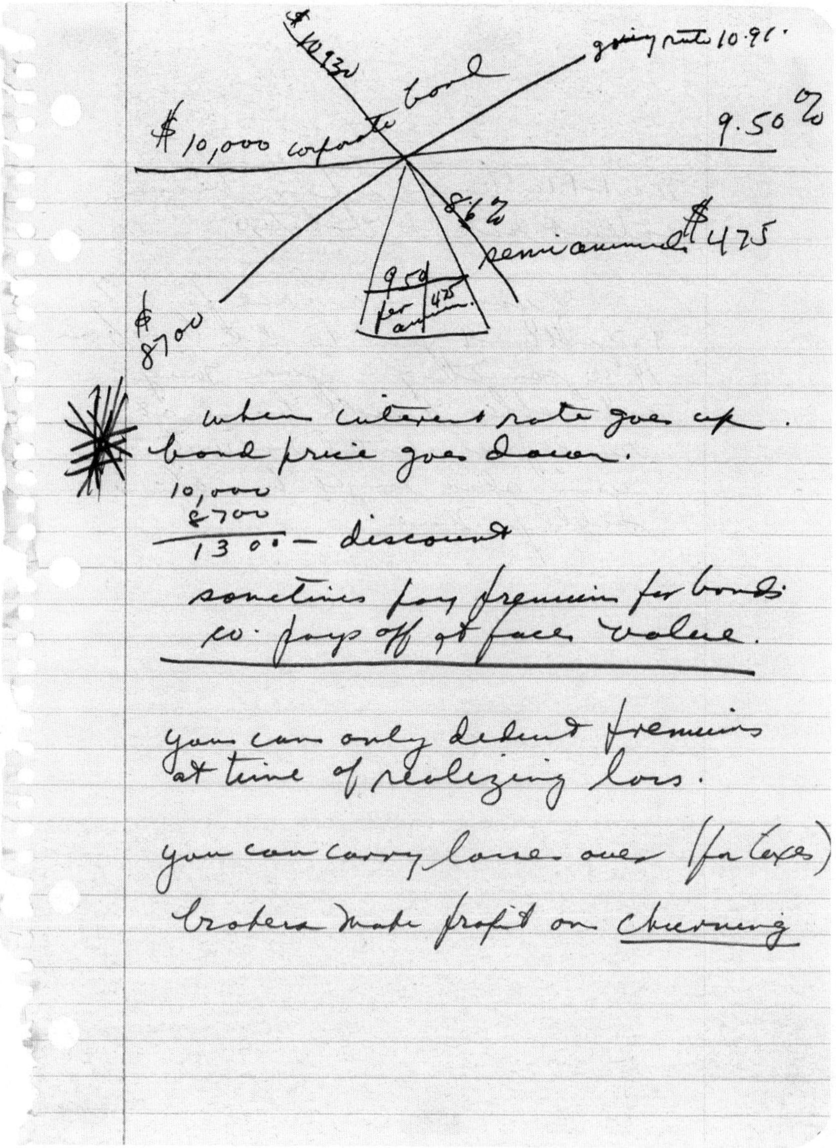

$10,932

going rate 10.91

$10,000 corporate bond

9.50%

8½%

semi annual $475

950 per annum

475 semi

$8700

when interest rate goes up. bond price goes down.

10,000
8700
1300 – discount

sometimes pay premium for bonds: co. pays off at face value.

you can only deduct premiums at time of realizing loss.

you can carry losses over (for taxes)

brokers make profit on churning

Money-advice note from Mom.

Schiaparelli's final creation.

Audrey's headpiece was modeled on a Schiaparelli hat.

AUDREY VOLK

November 24, 2001

15 Old House Lane
Chappaqua, NY 10515

My Dear Senator Clinton,

I have been a staunch admirer of yours for the last decade. You have always had the best interest of your fellow countrymen at heart and have presented yourself with the utmost dignity in every situation. Added to this is the wonderful, protective caring you and your husband have lavished on your beloved daughter.

One of my wonderful daughters has written this extremely well received memoir. It encompasses a period of New York history from a very intimate point of view but nonetheless gives the reader a real sense of the city (as it was) that is such an integral part of the state you represent.

I hope you have great pleasure reading this book.

Best wishes always.

Sincerely,

Audrey Volk

7107 MONTRICO DRIVE • BOCA RATON, FLORIDA • 33433
PHONE: (561) 338-7897 • FAX: (561) 750-0832

My mother remained in my corner till the end.

chapter twenty

Reflection

No book is the same twice.

No person stays the same between readings of that book.

The book changes because the person changes. The book you've just finished reading, this one, whether you liked it or not, has changed you. This book, if you started from page one right now, you'd notice new things because of the accreted fresh experience of having read the book. It would be different to you. It can't not.

I buy a 1954 copy of *Shocking Life* on eBay, and fifty-seven years after first reading it, read it again. What I missed when I was ten. I picked and chose, culled what I needed, the rest blurred by. I was on the edge of the lip of the cusp of the brink of puberty then, the age when I was primed to question my mother, to judge her, to stand back enough to see what I didn't like about her, to weigh the woman she ordained me to be against what I didn't want to be, what I *couldn't* be even if I'd wanted to. Her expectations had so little to do with my natural abilities or interests except for what she called my "strong point," the ability to draw. No matter how many lessons I took at Claremont Stables or how many classes at Madame Svoboda's, I would never master the basics of horsemanship or ballet. And I would never be a great beauty. On the other hand, I would be free to be something else, something that wasn't a birthright, something I made myself. I wanted to be good at something I earned. Beauty wasn't earned.

Children have their own logic and it's airtight. They know so little, what they believe to be true is unchallenged by experience. Intense young readers find the book they need when they need it. In an essay called "Essential Books of One's Life," Bruno Bettelheim writes: "Books lie in wait for our readiness." A book is influential to a child when the child has a "strong personal stake" in it. Cecil's books were meaningless to me. Puzzling, comic in a "People do *that*?" kind of way. Titillating with no place for that titillation to go. But with Schiap, I pounced. I needed her to deflate my all-powerful mother and she did. *Shocking Life* is not a great work of art. But it was the right book at the right time. It armed me to separate. It provided the transformative jolt. Schiap gave me an alternative way to be.

If I hadn't come across Schiap, chances are I would have found what I needed in another book. I was primed for a shock that could open up the world. It might have been another book my mother read. Or it might have been one we read for school, *George Washington Carver* by Camilla Wilson. As soon as I finished it, I read it again. George Washington Carver, the man who invented more than three hundred things to do with peanuts: peanut glue, peanut bleach, peanut coffee, peanut milk, peanut rubber, peanut lipstick, peanut ink, peanut shaving cream, peanut linoleum, peanut mayonnaise, peanut polish, paper, plastic, pavement and paint. Did everything have the potential to be something else? I knew it did. Didn't my sister dab toothpaste on her pimples? Didn't my paternal grandfather make his name by recycling the detritus from buildings he tore down? Didn't Picasso make a she-goat out of a basket and a baboon out of a toy car?

George Washington Carver made his own life. If he could, why couldn't I? A year after reading his biography, I'd be reading *The Scarlet Letter*, Jane Austen and *Jane Eyre*. But I already had Schiap. I already had my woman who made her own way.

For many events in life, you're more prepared than you know you are. How lucky I was to come across *Shocking Life* when I did. The people who made my two favorite pieces of art were Schiap's friends. From weekly painting lessons at the Museum of Modern Art, then the Met, then the Albert Pels School of Art on West Seventy-first Street, I was used to looking at pictures. Duchamp's irreverence speaks to young people. The Museum of Modern Art had one of his instruction pieces: *To Be Looked At (From the Other Side of the Glass) with One Eye, Close To, for Almost an Hour.* If you could stay the course, keep your eye glued to the lens in the assemblage for an hour, everything you saw turned upside down. A bicycle wheel impaled on a stool? Would your bike ever look the same? And what kid doesn't fall for Dalí's *The*

Persistence of Memory? Go there today and you'll see a clutch of gaping children holding their mothers' hands. Seeing what can't happen rendered in photographic verisimilitude? Time melts? Sand and sea solidify? And here was this woman who was their good friend. Who collaborated with Duchamp and Dalí by making things real that could exist only in a dream: a jacket with drawers for pockets. An evening bag that lights the way. Humans caught in a web.

I did not discuss *Shocking Life* with my mother but on finishing the book, began to see her differently, comparing the brilliant and opinionated Schiap to the brilliant and opinionated Audrey. My intent was not subversive. I was private and watchful. I needed to plot my own course. Audrey and Schiap had enough in common that I could risk comparisons. Both were educated. Both were working mothers ahead of their time, pre–women's movement. Both were imposing figures. Both were secretive. Both were hot-tempered and charismatic and crazy about clothes. Their opinions were sought. Reading was vital to them. They were brusque. Both disdained fat people and were moody. Moodiness was their acnestis—the part of an animal's back the animal can't scratch. That said, their differences were profound: Audrey loved being a wife. Being Mrs. Volk was her primary identity. Schiap, despite many opportunities, chose not to marry again. Audrey was the hostess in our family restaurant and a whiz at saving money. Schiap, at one time the best-known couturier in the world, made and lost millions, then made them again. Relatives moved into our home to ride out nervous breakdowns. Nurturing was not Schiap's interest or forte. Audrey was blinkered by convention. Schiap used shock to mask shyness.

Beauty was Audrey's main arena. Schiap was born with a constellation of moles on her face. Instead of hiding them, she designed a Big Dipper brooch with diamonds for stars and flaunted it. That pin alone was revelatory, the idea of extolling what others considered a problem, turning that problem into an asset. I loved that.

Where Audrey baffled, Schiap was clear and direct. Schiap was feminine, yet she was a first-rate athlete, ran a business, competed openly with men. The woman who invented sportswear wouldn't dream of throwing a race so a boy could win. She was daring. She got ideas and midwifed them to reality. She was alive to newness. She elected her affinities. I felt this in a way I couldn't put into words at ten.

Audrey's rules stretched the limit of the bearable. I watched my sister go down again and again. It wound up being good that I had trouble in school. When people expect less of you, you get a shot at doing what you want. Closing the covers of *Shocking Life,* I looked at Audrey with a fresh eye. There had to be more than one way to be a woman and if there was more than one way, chances were there were many. It was possible: A mother could be wrong about what was best for her child.

Raising me wasn't easy. I lived in a high-pitched state of excitement over nothing in particular. I was late. I forgot. I "time-traveled" in conversation. People threw up their hands. We choose our influences. Audrey's disappointments in me stopped being my disappointments in me. Schiap planted the idea that imagination trumped beauty, that being different might be a virtue. When she was my age, Schiap also performed dismally in school, had a gorgeous older sister, was considered exasperating and yet she managed to live a full-blown life, a life of invention and accomplishment. If Schiap, who had so many of the problems I had at ten, could turn out all right, I reasoned I could too.

Rereading *Shocking Life,* it's easy to see why it hit so hard. But I'm struck by how differently I see Schiap now. I still admire her and am awed by her work. That hasn't changed. But how on earth did I miss her profound melancholia? "Many men admire strong women, but they do not love them. Some women have achieved a combination of strength and tenderness, but most of those who have wanted to walk alone have, in the course of the game, lost their happiness." A woman's happiness depended on a man? That sailed right over my head. Also missed entirely on first reading: Schiap thought about killing herself. When I was ten, her black spells seemed romantic, exciting, a function of her creativity, like Van Gogh's—the purview of a genius. It didn't register that when Schiap was growing up she hid under the table and cried at her own birthday parties. By fifteen, Audrey knew how not to be hurt. She made herself emotionally impregnable. Schiap remained an open wound: "But who can define this kind of sorrow, that invades the soul like lead and bruises the body." Or "Always in my moments of success I am overcome by a sense of detachment, a feeling of insecurity, a knowledge that so much is futile—and a particular sadness." And "A malignant force was working against Schiap. . . . She had always been pursued by jealousy." Jealous? Schiap? Of whom? All that flew over my ten-year-old head. And so did the fact that Elsa Schiaparelli was a terrible mother. She spent Gogo's childhood getting rid of her.

The newborn was shipped to a nurse in Connecticut while Schiap looked for work in New York. When it was discovered that Gogo had polio, she was sent to a Parisian suburb to live with a doctor who administered painful electrical treatments with a *méchante boîte.* "I was deeply affected at having to leave her so very young, just at the moment when a child begins like a bud to take the color of the flower, with strangers, knowing that she would have to go through great pain." No viable treatments were available in the capital of France? At seven, Gogo departed for boarding schools in Switzerland and, except for vacations, never lived with her mother again. Schiap's five years with Gogo's father were a reconciliation to the loss of mattering. She makes clear that no one, even her daughter, could bring up his name. Gogo knew nothing about de Kerlor, not even what he looked like, until she was sixteen and a friend of Schiap's took her aside and showed her a photo. Particularly terrifying now that I have three grandchildren under the age of one: "Gogo . . . was an endearing, laughing child, never minding if she were left alone. . . . It was difficult to take her out as I had no perambulator." A newborn "never minding if she were left alone"? I glossed right over that. And there was no way of knowing, when I was ten, that two of Schiap's biographers would reveal she wasn't the fourteen-year-old wunderkind she claimed to be. When Schiap's book of erotic poems was published she was, in fact, twenty-one.

I missed that like Audrey, Schiap was supercritical: Meeting Gogo in London for a weekend, "I was quite stupefied by the sight of her. . . . She stood in front of me like an oaf, a graceless, puffed-up, fat, and very ugly girl." She complained about Gogo's "backfish" look, German slang for a teenage girl, an anonymous slab of fish that can be baked or fried. She wasn't there when Gogo married or gave birth. I didn't see that fifty-seven years ago. But, writing this now, I can't help pondering how Schiap's drive for financial security defined her idea of motherhood. Schiap had known extreme deprivation. Given the socioeconomic climate at the time, could she have achieved what she did and been a decent mother too? Is it fair to judge someone today by a social context acceptable eighty years ago? Is it fair to judge Schiap's use of endangered animals before they were endangered? Providing well for Gogo outweighed being together. My mother drove me nuts but she was there. She made herself a necessary person. I was a priority and I knew it.

Walking downtown on Fifth Avenue, I notice a dead bird in the street. So many cars have driven over the pigeon, it looks like an Anselm Kiefer painting. At Eighty-second Street, a three-block line snakes down the steps of the Met, all the way to the Eighty-fifth Street transverse, then swings back six blocks along Fifth Avenue down to Seventy-ninth. Thousands of people are waiting for the Metropolitan Museum to open. There wasn't a line like this for Vermeer or Scythian gold. Not for the Egyptians or Matisse. It's eight-twenty. At nine-thirty, the doors to *Savage Beauty*, the exhibition of the clothes and accessories of Alexander McQueen, will open. Coming toward me, a man pushes a metal rack along the pavement. Hangers are hung with what looks like newspapers. As he draws closer, I see they're dresses made out of *The New York Times*, elaborate dresses with pleated skirts, panniers and ruffs. Schiap made clothes out of silk printed with her newspaper reviews. On *The Times* Web site, Bill Cunningham, the great chronicler of fashion, comments on the McQueen show: "Schiaparelli showed all of this in a mad fling before World War II." Then he adds, "It's happening everywhere all over again!"

I see the show. I see it three times. And yes, Schiap did do all of it first: anatomical dresses, hats as masks, the matador as muse, pagoda shoulders, the human exoskeleton, the circus, industrial painting, taxidermy, the eroticism of death, feathers, feathers, feathers and flowers, flowers, flowers. And tartan. (Schiap and McQueen were both part Scot.) "You've got to know the rules to break them," McQueen said. "That's what I'm here for, to demolish the rules but to keep the tradition." Both were driven by anarchy. Both reveled in the Surrealist obsession with metamorphosis. Both brought theatricality to the everyday. Both tortured unorthodox materials into something unimaginable and dreamlike to take your breath away. Clothes with head-on visual impact. Clothes that snatch you into their world and force a response. Clothes that meet André Breton's maxim: "Beauty will be convulsive or will not be at all." The following year, the Met has a Schiap/Prada show and Schiap's influence pervades every inch of it.

Walking down the hallway leading to her bedroom she passes her self-portrait. She'd given it to her mother but now Audrey is dead and her self-portrait is hers again. Audrey had good things to say about her work but she was not the kind of mother who would hang a daughter's painting simply because it was done by her daughter. The self-portrait is based on a grid, 660 squares meticulously drawn on white hot-press Bainbridge board with a Koh-i-Noor Rapidograph and Higgins India ink. The idea was to fill in as few of the squares as possible, each with transparent color, and still render a recognizable face. As each square was filled, she stepped back to see if that was enough to be her. She kept filling one square at a time, stepping back, then filling in another square, until she began to see herself emerge. That was when she stopped. She had in mind what Schiap's friend and collaborator Alberto Giacometti wanted to do: Take away as much as you can while still communicating what a thing is. Pare it to its essence. (Although now, when she looks at the portrait, she knows she could have reduced it more.) She was interested not only in the power of reduction. She was interested in how much the viewer was willing to participate to make an object (in this case, a particular face) recognizable. How willing is a viewer to fill in the blanks? Georgia O'Keeffe is not mentioned in *Shocking Life* but Schiap was good friends with Alfred Stieglitz and actively participated in life at his galleries. Had Schiap known O'Keeffe? Though no biographies suggest they crossed paths, how could they not have met? O'Keeffe was living with Stieglitz in New York when Schiap made his acquaintance. They became good friends. She likes thinking Georgia and Schiap knew each other and respected each other's work. Her self-portrait reminds her of what Georgia O'Keeffe said about her adobe home in Abiquiu: "I want nothing I can get along without."

Schiap wanted to see who could throw it the farthest. Risk-taking to her was a form of expression. Perhaps what drew me to Schiap most was her ability to run with an idea, to tweak it almost beyond endurance, something Audrey could not do. Something, in fact, Audrey did not approve of. What Audrey wanted for me above all was the antithesis of magic. What she wanted for me was a life safe from disappointment. If I asked my mother for eye hooks to make a fishing pole, she'd give me twenty reasons why it wouldn't work. It was her job to be practical and put an end to harebrained schemes. She was an idea-quasher, a mocker, a fierce opponent of invention, a dream-killer, all in the name of guardianship. But I felt alive when I was dreaming. Trying to make a dream real was better than failure. You got ideas from failure. Failure was never not interesting.

I used to not know how to feel about my mother. What word has more interpretations than "love"? "Love" means something different to every person who says it and every person who hears it. "Love" has as many meanings as there are people. I know that now. And I know that every big event in a life—work, love, children, loss—is filtered through the lens of what you need to see at that time—even when you are ten.

Schiap made clear the value of probing an idea, of turning it over, playing with it like a squirrel with a nut. She revered meaning. She took joy in her work. She helped me learn how to see, the ripe kaleidoscopic pure pleasure of looking. I take her with me. Daydreaming, to Audrey, was perilous, something to "snap out of." Being original, being yourself to my beautiful beloved mother was not safe. Being original, being yourself to Elsa Schiaparelli was life-giving. She made a hat out of a shoe. Reading that at ten, I knew: Anything is possible.

It's easy to pick out George Washington Carver.
He always wore a peanut-flower boutonniere.

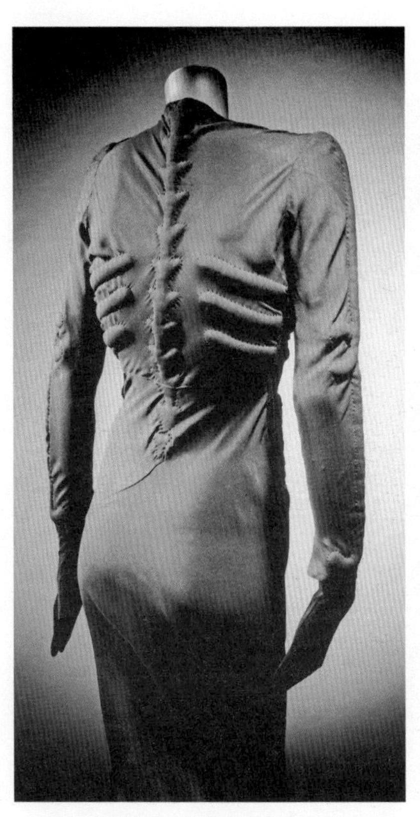

Schiap's Skeleton Dress.

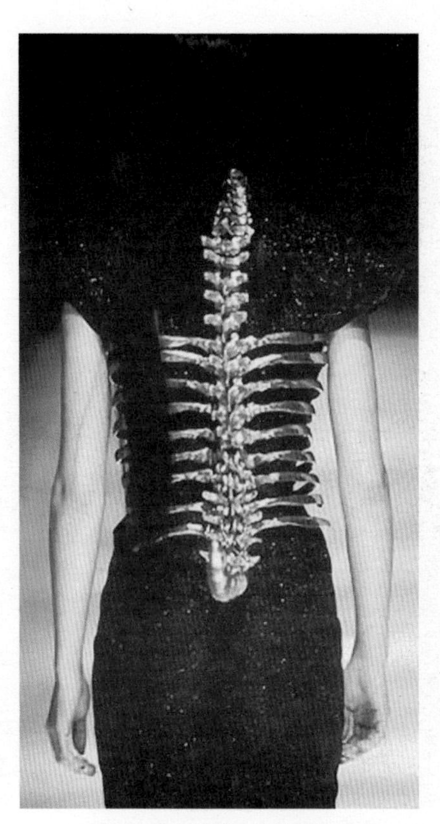

Alexander McQueen's Spine
Corset by Shaun Leane.

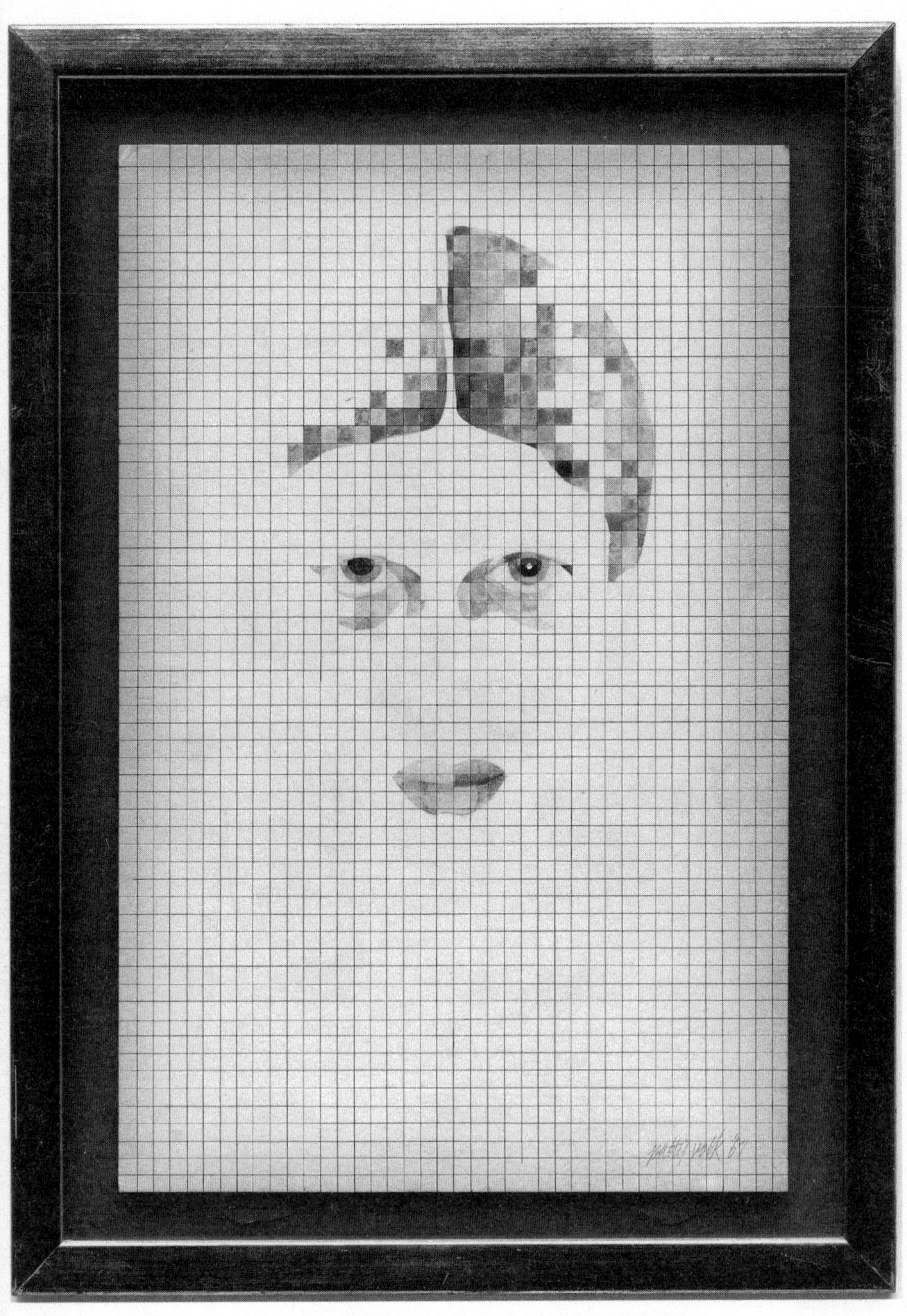

"I want nothing I can get along without."

Schiap and O'Keeffe.
I imagined two such extraordinary artists were friends.

Transformative Books

the transformative book
of ten people in this book

Audrey Morgen Volk	*Marie Antoinette* by Stefan Zweig
Cecil Sussman Volk	*White Fang* by Jack London
Jo Ann Volk Lederman	*The Good Earth* by Pearl S. Buck
Marcel Proust	Galland's *The Arabian Nights*
Adolf Hitler	*The Riddle of the Jew's Success* by F. Roderich-Stoltheim
Elvis Presley	*The Prophet* by Kahlil Gibran
Polly Ann Lieban Morgen	*Pollyanna* by Eleanor H. Porter
Hillary Clinton	*1984* by George Orwell
Elsa Schiaparelli	*The Rubaiyat of Omar Khayyam*
Mattie Sylvia Lee Myles Weems Watts	The Holy Bible

the transformative book
of ten other people

Michelle Obama	*Song of Solomon* by Toni Morrison
Barack Obama	*The Power Broker* by Robert Caro
Robert Caro	*Captain Horatio Hornblower* by C. S. Forester
Nora Ephron	*A Little Princess* by Frances Hodgson Burnett
Marilyn Monroe	*How Stanislavsky Directs* by Michael Gorchakov

Oprah Winfrey	*The Bluest Eye* by Toni Morrison
Toni Morrison	*Pride and Prejudice* by Jane Austen
Steve Jobs	*Moby-Dick* by Herman Melville
Steven Spielberg	*Treasure Island* by Robert Louis Stevenson
Ludwig van Beethoven	*Lives of Noble Grecians and Romans* by Plutarch

Acknowledgments

Thank you, Jo Ann Volk Lederman, Joel Conarroe, Dr. Martin Bergmann, Gail Gregg, Molly Haskell, Frances Kiernan, Lily Tuck, Amy Hempel, Sidney Offit, Brad Gooch, Anka Muhlstein, Stephen Deutsch, Etheleen and Allen Staley, Karen Broderick, Robin Desser, Jennifer Kurdyla, Gloria Loomis, Julia Masnik, Ken Leach, Sara Cedar Miller, Harold Reed, Kelly Gonda, Dilys Blum, Harold Koda, Emanuelle Beuvin, Leslie Chin and the New York Society Library. A particular thank-you to Master New York Map-Maker John Tauranac, whose perfect images I made less perfect. "Thank you" barely scratches the surface for my friend Mark Woods and his photographs. Bless the Guggenheim Foundation for a solid year of research and writing. And for their essential and generous hospitality, bless the Corporation of Yaddo, Susan Calhoun and Charlie Moss.

Bibliography

Addressing the Century: 100 Years of Art and Fashion. White Dove Press, 1998.

Alexander McQueen: Savage Beauty. Metropolitan Museum of Art, 2011.

Baudot, François. *Elsa Schiaparelli*. Universe Publishing, 1997.

———. *Fashion & Surrealism*. Assouline, 2001.

Baxter-Wright, Emma. *The Little Book of Schiaparelli*. Carlton Books, 2012.

Blum, Dilys E. *Shocking!: The Art and Fashion of Elsa Schiaparelli*. Philadelphia Museum of Art, in association with Yale University Press, 2003.

Charles-Roux, Edmonde. *Chanel*. Collins Harvill, 1989.

Fashion Book, The. Phaidon, 1998.

Kurth, Peter. *Isadora: A Sensational Life*. Little Brown, 2001.

Lacroix, Christian, Patrick Mauries, and Oliver Saillard. *Christian Lacroix on Fashion*. Thames & Hudson, 2007.

Marcel Duchamp Étant Donnés: Manual of Instructions. Philadelphia Museum of Art, in association with Yale University Press, 2009.

Mehring, Christine. *Wols Photographs*. Busch-Reisinger Museum, 1999.

O'Keeffe, Georgia. *Some Memories of Drawing*. University of New Mexico Press, 1974.

Pile, Stephen. *The Incomplete Book of Failures: The Official Hand-*

book of the Not-Terribly-Good Club of Great Britain. E. P. Dutton, 1979.

Rubin, William. *Dada, Surrealism, and Their Heritage*. Museum of Modern Art, 1968.

Schiaparelli, Elsa. *Shocking Life*. E. P. Dutton, 1954.

Tomkins, Calvin. *Duchamp: A Biography*. Henry Holt, 1996.

Turner, Elizabeth Hutton. *In the American Grain*. Counterpoint, 1995.

Tuska, Jon. *The Films of Mae West*. The Citadel Press, 1983.

Vaughan, Hal. *Sleeping with the Enemy: Coco Chanel's Secret War*. Alfred A. Knopf, 2011.

West, Mae. *Goodness Had Nothing to Do with It*. Belvedere Publishers, 1959.

White, Palmer. *Elsa Schiaparelli: Empress of Paris Fashion*. Rizzoli International, 1986.

Wood, Ghislaine. *Surreal Things: Surrealism and Design*. V&A Publications, 2007.

Zohm, Volker. *Art Fashion*. Mondi Textil GmbH, 1991.

Illustration Credits

Unless otherwise noted, all photographs are from the author's personal collection. We have tried to identify all copyright holders; in case of an oversight and upon notification to the publisher, corrections will be made in subsequent printings.

Page xi: [Elsa Schiaparelli, half-length portrait, facing front], 1952. New York World-Telegram and the Sun Newspaper Photograph Collection (Library of Congress).

Page 11: Courtesy Evertt Collection, Inc.

Page 12: Salvador Dalí, Spanish, 1904–1989, *Mae West's Face Which May be Used as a Surrealist Apartment*, 1934–1935, gouache, with graphite, on commercially printed magazine page, 283 x 178 mm (sight), Gift of Mrs. Charles B. Goodspeed, 1949.517, The Art Institute of Chicago. © 2008 Salvador Dalí, Fundació Gala-Salvador Dalí, Artists Rights Society (ARS), New York 2012.

Page 13: Bridgeman Art Library Limited. © Salvador Dalí, Fundació Gala-Salvador Dalí, Artists Rights Society (ARS), New York 2012.

Page 14: © Imperial War Museum (CH 83) (detail).

Page 15: *Vogue*, December 1937.

Page 27: Photographic compositing by Mark Woods (Mark-Woods.com).

Page 28: *(top)* Courtesy Ken Leach; *(bottom)* Modern Library logo is used by permission of Random House, Inc.

Page 29: Jack Lake Productions, Inc.

Page 30: Design by John Tauranac © Tauranac, Ltd., 2012. All Rights Reserved. Printed with Permission.

Page 38: Teddy Piaz.

Page 39: *(top)* Collection Clo Fleiss, Paris. © 2012 Artists Rights Society

(ARS), New York / ProLitteris, Zurich. Image editing by Mark Woods (Mark-Woods.com); *(bottom)* © 2012 Artists Rights Society (ARS), New York / ProLitteris, Zurich. Image editing by Mark Woods (Mark-Woods.com).

Page 40: Philadelphia Museum of Art: Gift of Mme Elsa Schiaparelli, 1969. © 2012 Artists Rights Society (ARS), New York / ProLitteris, Zurich. Image editing by Mark Woods (Mark-Woods.com).

Page 41: Elsa Schiaparelli, 12/6/1939. © 2012 The Associated Press.

Page 42: Photograph by Mark Woods (Mark-Woods.com).

Page 44: Photograph by Mark Woods (Mark-Woods.com).

Page 45: © Norbert Nowotsch.

Page 52: Photograph by Mark Woods (Mark-Woods.com).

Page 54: Vanni / Art Resource, NY.

Page 55: Alinari / Art Resource, NY. Photographic compositing by Mark Woods (Mark-Woods.com).

Page 56: *(top and bottom)* Photographs by Mark Woods (Mark-Woods.com).

Page 66: Droits Reserves Schiaparelli archives.

Page 67: Philadelphia Museum of Art: Gift of the Cassandra Foundation, 1969. © 2012 Artists Rights Society (ARS), New York / ADAGP, Paris / Succession Marcel Duchamp.

Page 68: *(top)* Philadelphia Museum of Art: Gift of the Cassandra Foundation, 1969. © 2012 Artists Rights Society (ARS), New York / ADAGP, Paris / Succession Marcel Duchamp.

Page 81: © 2012 Man Ray Trust / Artists Rights Society (ARS), New York / ADAGP, Paris.

Page 82: Salvador Dalí *(left)* Spanish, 1904–1989, *Venus de Milo with Drawers,* 1936. Painted plaster with metal pulls and mink pompons, 38⅝ x 12¾ x 13⅜ in. (98 x 32.5 x 34 cm). Through prior gift of Mrs. Gilbert W. Chapman, 2005.424, The Art Institute of Chicago. © 2008 Salvador Dalí, Fundació Gala-Salvador Dalí, Artists Rights Society (ARS), New York 2012 (detail). *(right)* Model wearing a black wool coat with eight bureau-drawer pockets, inspired by Salvador Dalí, and a hat with a patent-leather fence on top, both by Schiaparelli (detail). Cecil Beaton © Condé Nast Archive / CORBIS. Photographic compositing by Mark Woods (Mark-Woods.com).

Page 83: Photofest.

Page 101: Bundesarchiv, Bild 102–11505 / photographer: unknown / License

CC-BY-SA 3.0, www.bundesarchiv.de/picture-archives. Photographic compositing by Mark Woods (Mark-Woods.com).

Page 102: Courtesy Mark McMunn, grandnephew of Cosme McMoon; *(inset)* © Lebrecht Music & Arts / The Image Works.

Page 103: Photograph by Mark Woods (Mark-Woods.com).

Page 104: Photograph by Mark Woods (Mark-Woods.com).

Page 105: Photograph by Mark Woods (Mark-Woods.com).

Page 116: © Philippe Halsman / Magnum Photos.

Page 117: *(top)* Photograph by Mark Woods (Mark-Woods.com); *(bottom)* Image copyright © The Metropolitan Museum of Art. Image Source: Art Resource, NY.

Page 125: Courtesy New York Public Library. Photographic compositing by Mark Woods (Mark-Woods.com).

Page 126: Image editing by Mark Woods (Mark-Woods.com).

Page 136: Philadelphia Museum of Art: Gift of Mme Elsa Schiaparelli, 1969.

Page 137: © V&A Images / Victoria and Albert Museum, London.

Page 138: *(top and bottom)* Photographs by Mark Woods (Mark-Woods .com).

Page 148: *(left)* © TIME, Inc.; *(right)* Photograph by Mark Woods (Mark -Woods.com).

Page 149: *(top left and right)* Photographs by Mark Woods (Mark-Woods .com); *(bottom left)* Photofest.

Page 150: Photo by John Phillips / Getty Images.

Page 152: Bridgeman Art Library Limited. © 2012 Man Ray Trust / Artists Rights Society (ARS), New York / ADAGP, Paris.

Page 153: *(top)* © 2012 Man Ray Trust / Artists Rights Society (ARS), New York / ADAGP, Paris; *(bottom)* © Sky & Telescope. All Rights Reserved. Used with permission. Image editing by Mark Woods (Mark-Woods .com).

Page 154: *(top)* Image copyright © The Metropolitan Museum of Art. Image Source: Art Resource, NY; *(bottom)* Schiaparelli, in a surrealistic mood, designs this red satin, visored evening cap with an elongated peephole for the eye. A diamond clip from Van Cleef & Arpels makes a weird eyebrow. Ca. 1936. © Bettmann / CORBIS.

Page 155: *(right and left)* Photograph and photographic compositing by Mark Woods (Mark-Woods.com).

Page 166: *(top and bottom)* Photographs by Mark Woods (Mark-Woods .com).

Page 175: Designed by John Tauranac © Tauranac, Ltd., 2000; Revised, 2012. All Rights Reserved. Printed with Permission.
Page 176: S.M. Productions.
Page 177: Photograph by Mark Woods (Mark-Woods.com).
Page 178: Photograph by Erika Blitzer.
Page 186: Schiaparelli family archive.
Page 199: Photograph by Mark Woods (Mark-Woods.com).
Page 200: Courtesy LALIQUE. © 2012 Artists Rights Society (ARS), New York / ADAGP, Paris.
Page 202: *(bottom)* Photograph by Mark Woods (Mark-Woods.com).
Page 203: *(top)* Photo by John Phillips / Time Life Pictures / Getty Images; *(bottom left and right)* Photograph by Gail Gregg.
Page 209: Kevin Schafer / Minden Pictures.
Page 218: Philadelphia Museum of Art, Archives: Gift of Jacqueline, Paul and Peter Matisse in memory of their mother, Alexina Duchamp. © 2012 Artists Rights Society (ARS), New York / ADAGP, Paris / Succession Marcel Duchamp.
Page 219: *(all)* Photographs by Mark Woods (Mark-Woods.com).
Page 220: CBS Photo Archive / Getty Images; *(inset)* Photo by Roland Schoor / Getty Images.
Page 235: Image copyright © The Metropolitan Museum of Art. Image Source: Art Resource, NY.
Page 238: Photograph by Mark Woods (Mark-Woods.com).
Page 251: Anatomy, 1930, by Man Ray. © 2012 Man Ray Trust / Artists Rights Society (ARS), New York / ADAGP, Paris.
Page 252: Photograph by Mark Woods (Mark-Woods.com).
Page 253: *(top and bottom)* © Martyn F. Chillmaid.
Page 254: Photograph by Mark Woods (Mark-Woods.com).
Page 255: Photograph by Mark Woods (Mark-Woods.com).
Page 269: *(left)* © V&A Images / Victoria and Albert Museum, London; *(right)* © firstVIEW.
Page 270: Photograph by Mark Woods (Mark-Woods.com).
Page 271: [Elsa Schiaparelli] Image copyright © The Metropolitan Museum of Art. Image Source: Art Resource, NY. Elsa Schiaparelli (detail) © Hulton-Deutsch Collection / CORBIS. Georgia O'Keeffe (detail) © Bettmann / CORBIS. [shoe hat] Digital Image © The Metropolitan Museum of Art / Licensed by SCALA / Art Resource, NY. Photographic compositing by Mark Woods (Mark-Woods.com).

Color Insert:

Page 1: Image copyright © The Metropolitan Museum of Art. Image Source: Art Resource, NY.

Page 2: Image copyright © The Metropolitan Museum of Art. Image Source: Art Resource, NY.

Page 3: *(top)* Image editing by Mark Woods (Mark-Woods.com); *(bottom)* Leslie Chin, Vintage Luxury.

Page 4: Photo Les Arts Décoratifs, Paris / Jean Tholance, tous droits réservés.

Acquisition/dépôt: Don Patricia Lopez-Willshaw, UFAC, 1966

ensemble 2 pièces robe; Elsa Schiaparelli, 1937, collection été (haute couture); soie satin imprimé ; soie crêpe ; crin résille (techn.) longueur (en cm) 157 tour de taille (en cm) 70 largeur aux épaules (en cm) 45 longueur manteau (en cm) 151 tour de taille (en cm) 64 tour de poitrine (en cm) 79 mode et textile (UFAC).

Page 5: © V&A Images / Victoria and Albert Museum, London.

Page 6: Philadelphia Museum of Art: Gift of Mme Elsa Schiaparelli, 1969. Image copyright © The Metropolitan Museum of Art. Image Source: Art Resource, NY. Image editing by Mark Woods (Mark-Woods.com).

Page 7: *(left)* Philadelphia Museum of Art: Gift of Mme Elsa Schiaparelli, 1969 Costume and Textiles; *(right)* Philadelphia Museum of Art: Gift of Mme Elsa Schiaparelli, 1969 Costume and Textiles.

Page 8: Image editing by John Muggenborg.

A Note on the Type

This book was set in Fairfield, a typeface designed by the distinguished American artist and engraver Rudolph Ruzicka (1883–1978). Ruzicka was born in Bohemia and came to America in 1894. He designed and illustrated many books, and was the creator of a considerable list of individual prints in a variety of techniques.

Composed by North Market Street Graphics,
Lancaster, Pennsylvania